My First
KANJI Book

Japanese Language and
Culture through Pictures

Bret Mayer

ナツメ社

Author / Bret Mayer
Born and raised in New Jersey, USA, Bret Mayer lives and works as a
certified Kanji Instructor in Hamamatsu, Shizuoka, Japan. In Autumn of
2012, Mayer became the first foreigner to pass the highest level of the
Japan Kanji Aptitude Test, completing every level the testing foundation
has to offer. In Spring of 2013, Mayer became a licensed Kanji Instructor
as recognized by Ritsumeikan University. Currently, he teaches kanji to both
Japanese and foreigners regularly on radio and TV programs and online.

Book Design
YORIFUJI Bunpei / ARAKAKI Yuko

Illustration
IDICHI Hiroyuki

Associate Editors
OFFICE303, Inc / ISHIMURA Meishuku

Editor
SAITO Masayuki (Natsume Shuppan Kikaku Co.,Ltd.)

My First Kanji Book
Japanese Language and Culture through Pictures
First Edition Jun 2016

Publisher
Natsumesha Co.,Ltd.
Natsumesha Bldg. 1F 1-52 Kanda-Jimbocho, Chiyoda-ku,
Tokyo, Japan 101-0051

Production
Natsume Shuppan Kikaku Co.,Ltd.

Printing
TOPPAN Colorer Inc.

We will replace the book if it has a manufacturing defect.
No part of this book may be reproduced in any form beyond the limits set
forth by copyright law without written permission from the publisher.
ISBN978-4-8163-6060-2   ©NATSUMESYA

Preface

The study of kanji can become very deep and complex. Multiple pronunciations, multiple forms and history that stretches back to ancient China. But don't worry about that now! This book is to introduce kanji characters as a form of communication to people who have used ABC's their whole life. The key is baby steps, daily exposure and the curiosity and motivation to keep moving forward.

Along the way, some characters are introduced in haiku form. It is my hope that this book can give the reader an appreciation of Japanese culture and inspire a love of kanji characters.

If you have any questions about the book, or just want to chat about kanji, feel free to contact me on Twitter (@BuSensei). I also have a video series on kanji study on YouTube (http://www.youtube.com/busensei) should you feel ready to get more in-depth.

For now, thank you so much for purchasing my book, and please... enjoy! Above all, kanji are FUN!

Bret Mayer

CONTENTS

Preface	3
Composition of the Book	4
STEP1	5
STEP2	75
STEP3	145
INDEX	201

Composition of the Book

STEP1-3

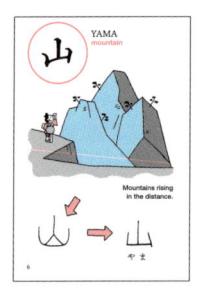

Many kanji developed from pictographic shapes, and even now, some kanji retain these elements.

This book introduces 200 characters by using illustrations (shown center page), which are based on these original pictographs (shown bottom left page).

Kanji in Haiku

Additionally, this book includes 6 haiku with illustrations of the scenes they depict.

Enjoy a slice of traditional Japanese culture as you learn kanji!

STEP1

Nature, the human body
and simple concepts.

YAMA
mountain

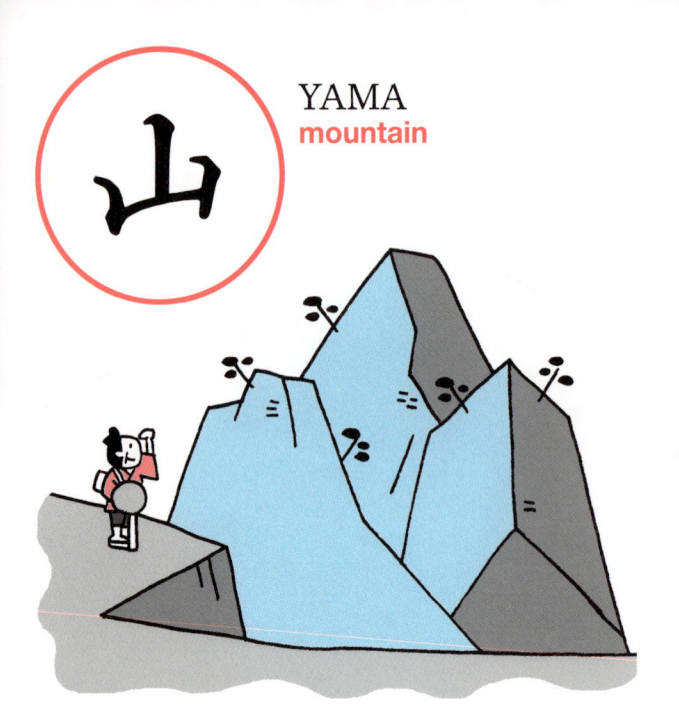

Mountains rising in the distance.

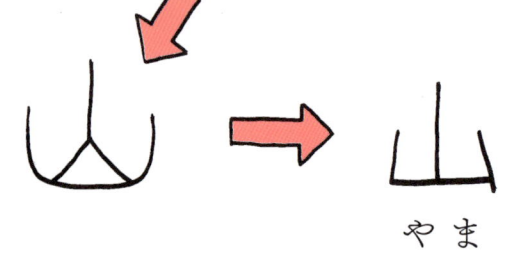

やま

KAWA
river

川

A fast-flowing river.

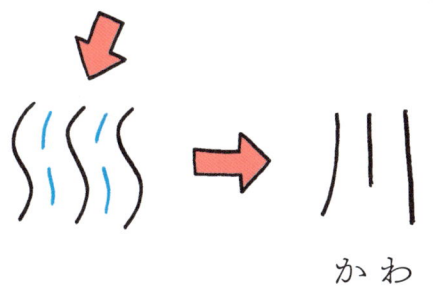

川

かわ

7

HI, NICHI
sun, day of the week, Sunday

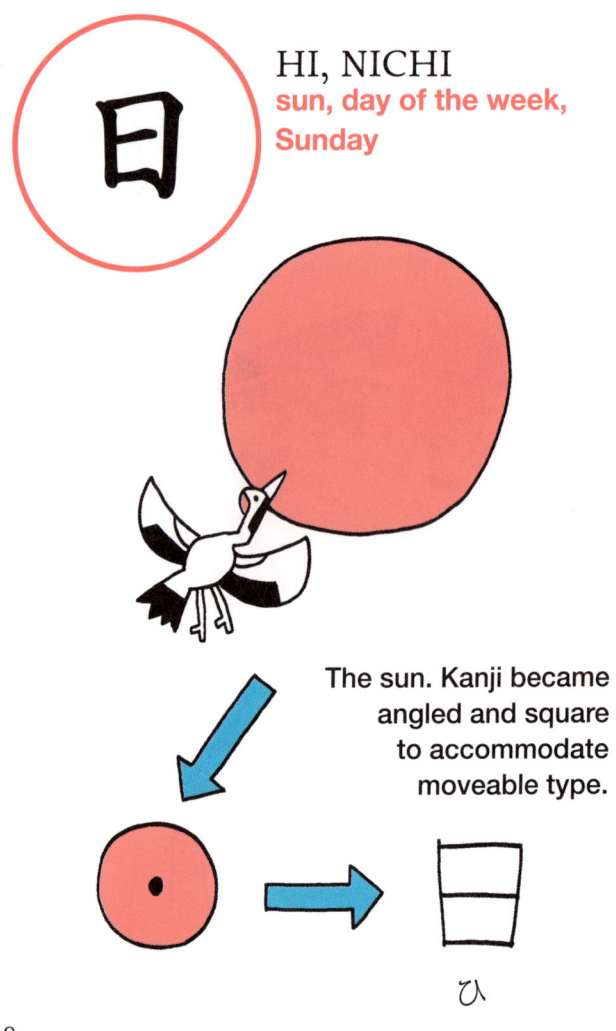

日

The sun. Kanji became angled and square to accommodate moveable type.

ひ

TSUKI, GETSU
moon, month, Monday

月

The moon.
To separate it from sun,
a crescent moon is used.

月
つき

水

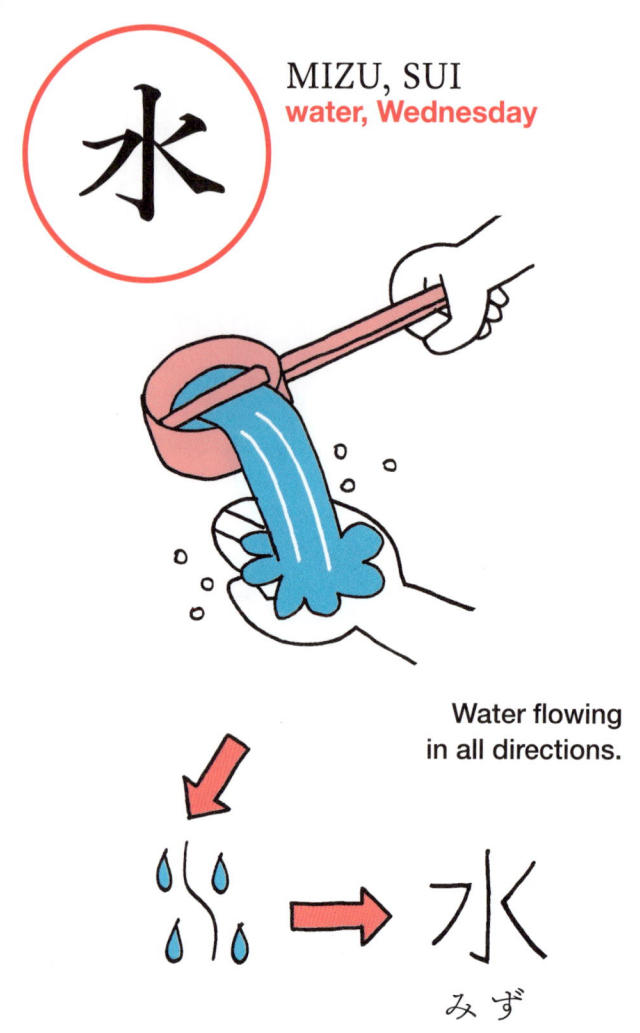

MIZU, SUI
water, Wednesday

Water flowing in all directions.

みず

KI, MOKU
tree, wood, Thursday

木

A tree with roots reaching down and braches spread to the sides.

き

石

ISHI
rock

A rock sitting at the base of a cliff.

いし

TSUCHI, DO
earth, soil, Saturday

土

A pile of dirt. The lines show height and width.

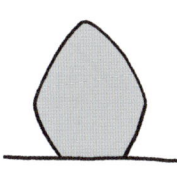

土
つち

金

KANE, KIN
money, gold, Friday

Two gold nuggets buried deep in the ground.

金 → 金

かね

14

HI, KA
fire, Tuesday

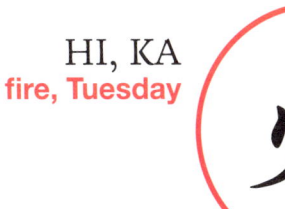

火

A roaring fire.

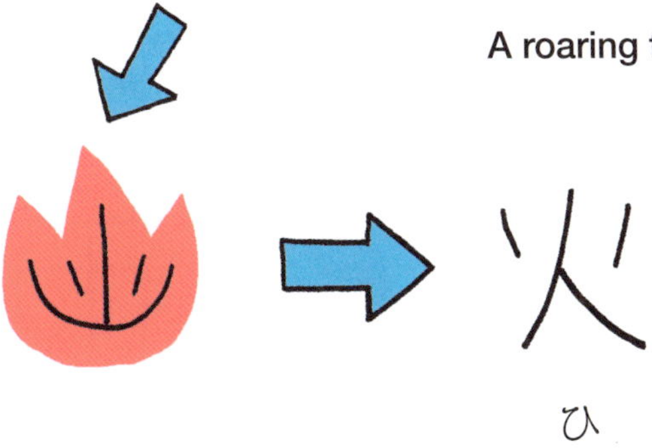

火

ひ

雨

AME
rain

Raindrops falling from clouds that cover the sky.

雨 → 雨
あめ

TA
rice field

田

A rice field divided into four sections.

た

目

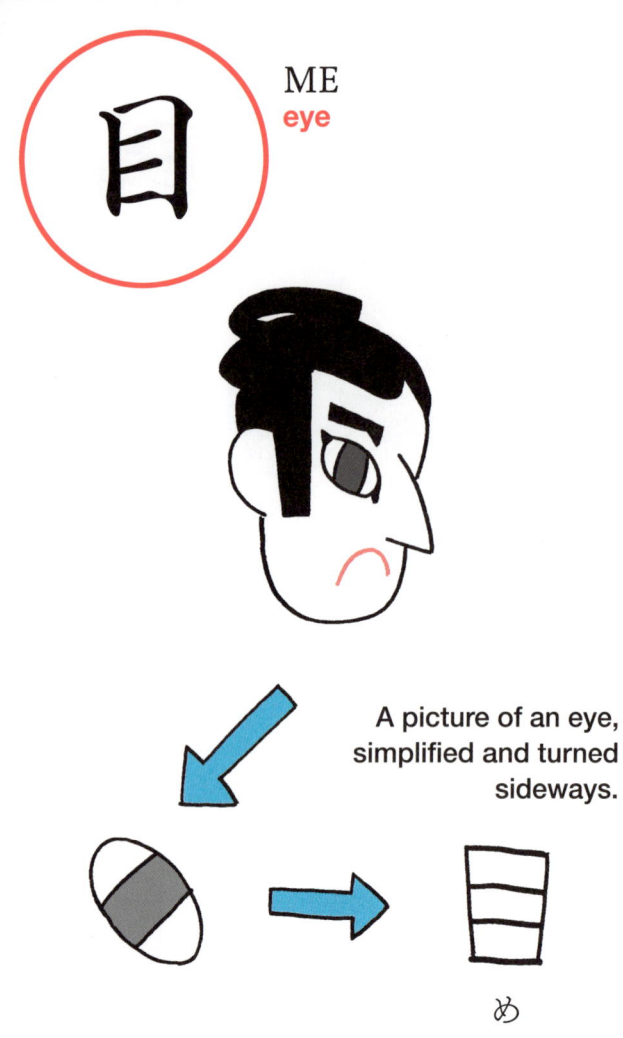

ME
eye

A picture of an eye, simplified and turned sideways.

め

MIMI
ear

耳

A drawing of the inside of an ear.

みみ

KUCHI
mouth

口

An open mouth.

くち

JI
self

自

A picture of a nose. Japanese point to their nose when referring to themselves.

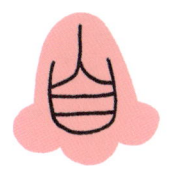

じ

手

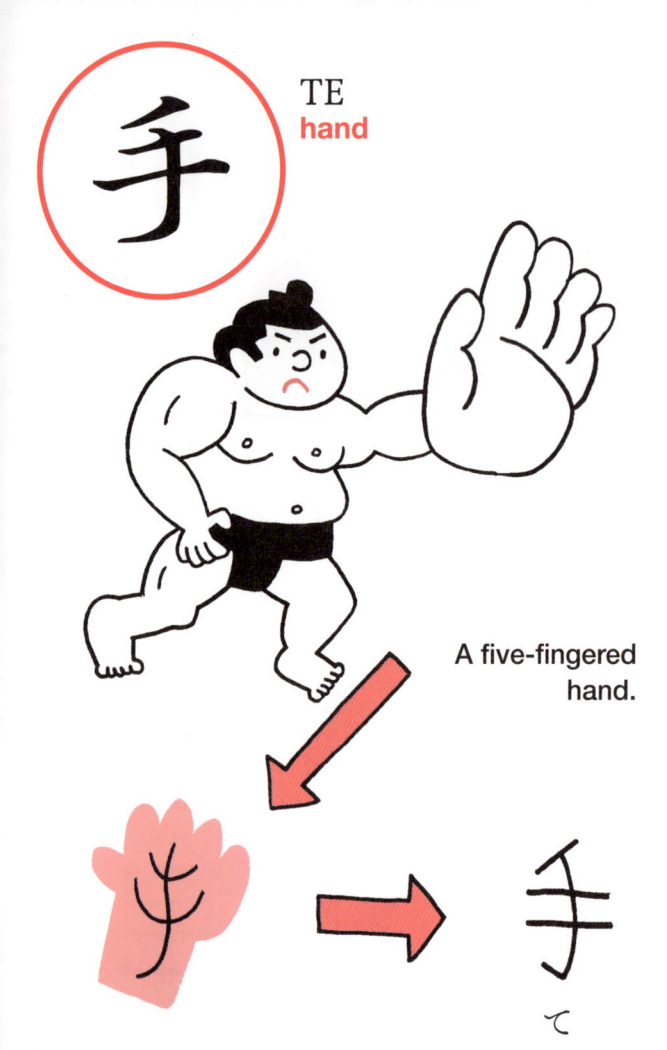

TE
hand

A five-fingered hand.

手
て

ASHI
leg, foot

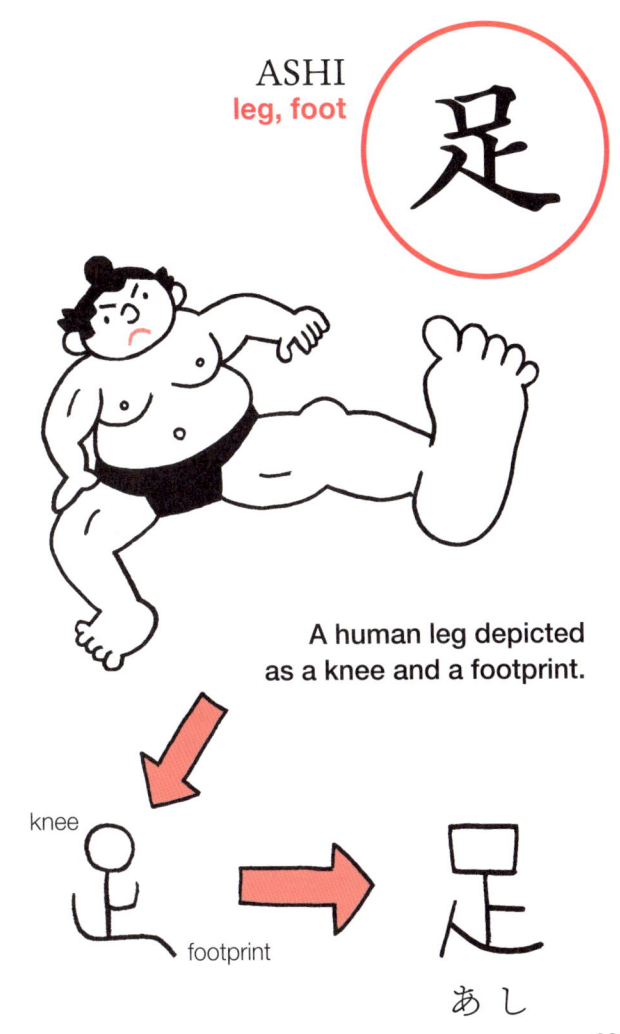

足

A human leg depicted as a knee and a footprint.

knee

footprint

→ 足
あし

CHIKARA
power, force

力

A person shows their power by flexing their muscly arm.

ちから

HA
tooth

歯

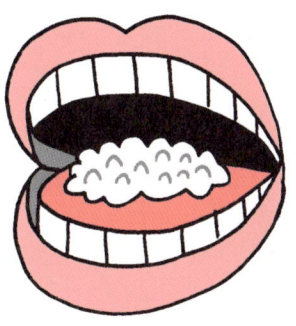

Rice stops in the mouth to be chewed by the teeth. Please chew with your mouth closed.

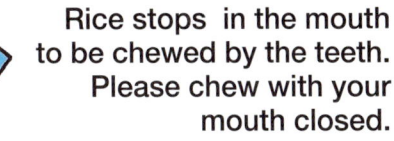

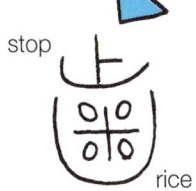

stop

rice

→ 歯

は

KOKORO
heart, mind

心

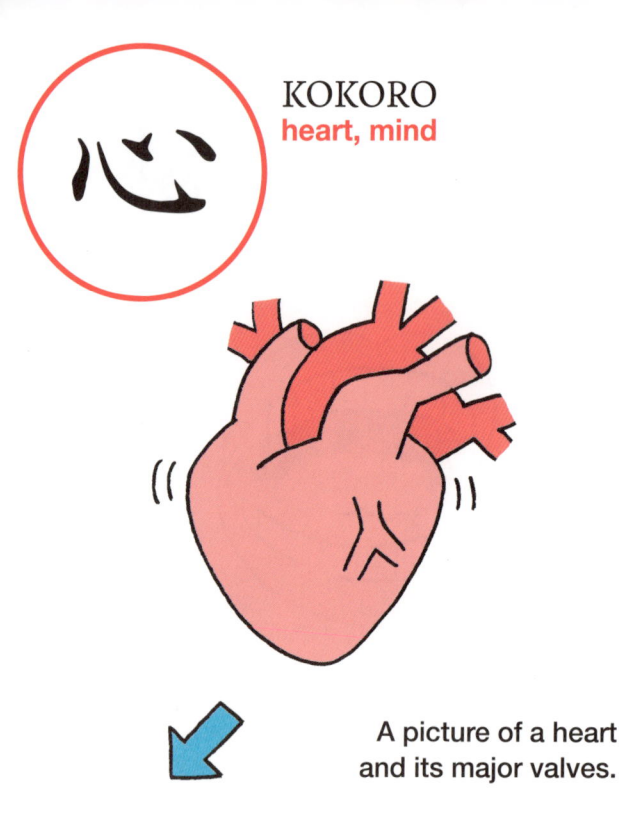

A picture of a heart and its major valves.

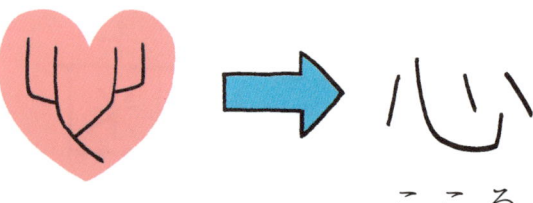

心
こころ

HITO
person

人

A person walking pictured from the side.

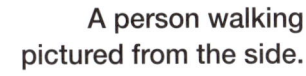

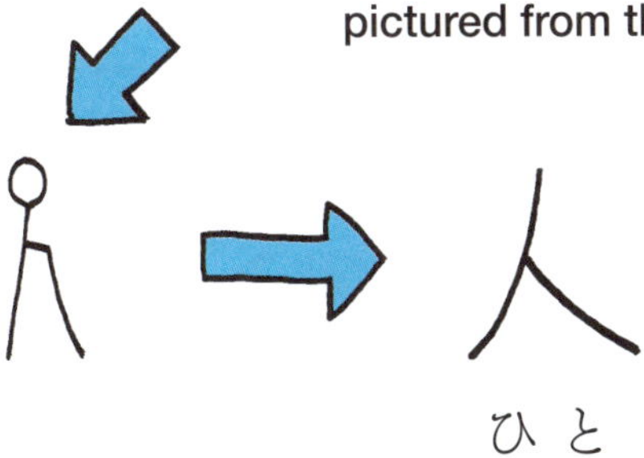

ひと

ON'NA
woman

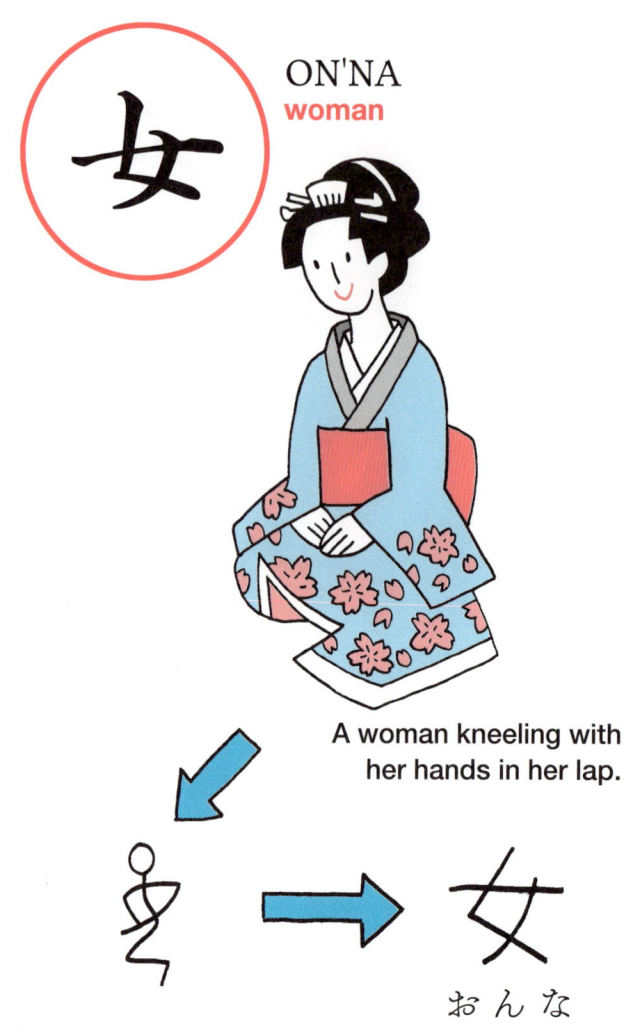

女

A woman kneeling with her hands in her lap.

おんな

KO
child

子

A child with arms outstretched.

子

こ

Kanji in Haiku

古池や
蛙飛び込む
水の音

31

Kanji

机 [tsukue] desk

窓 [mado] window

飛 [to-bu] jump

池 [ike] pond

葉 [ha] leaf

音 [oto] sound

蛙 [kawazu] frog

The illustration represents the scene of the following haiku.

furu　ike　ya
古 池 や

kawazu　to　bi　ko　mu
蛙 飛 び 込 む

mizu　no　oto
水 の 音

matsu　o　ba　sho
松 尾 芭 蕉

What it means.

An old pond
A frog jumps in
The sound of the water.

One quiet spring day, a frog jumps in a old pond. The sound breaks the silence briefly and then the pond regains its stillness.

骨

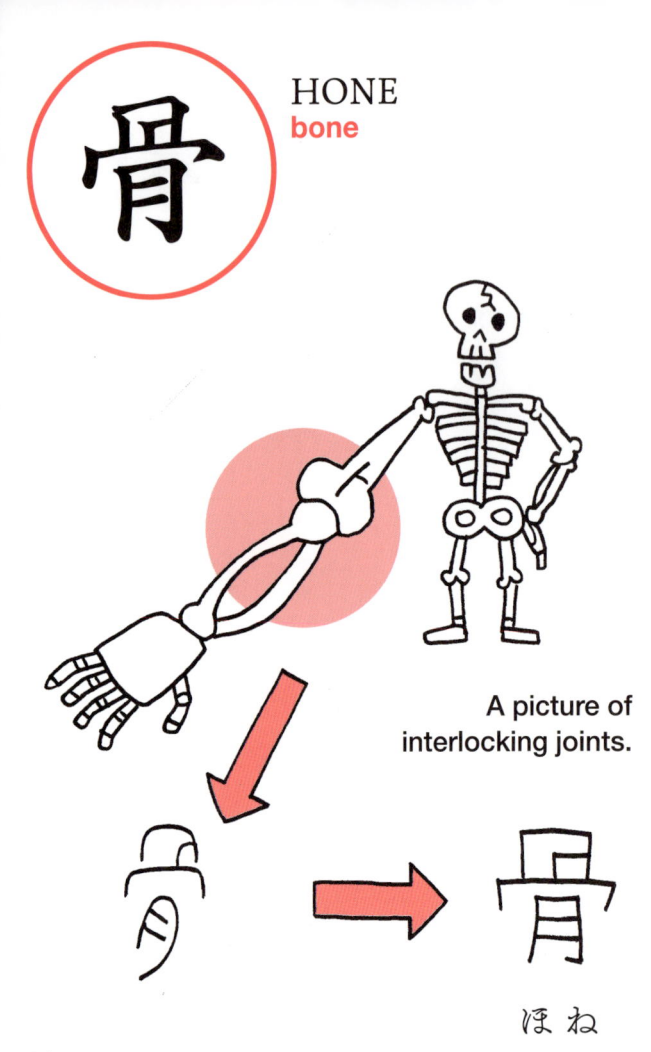

HONE
bone

A picture of interlocking joints.

ほね

INU
dog

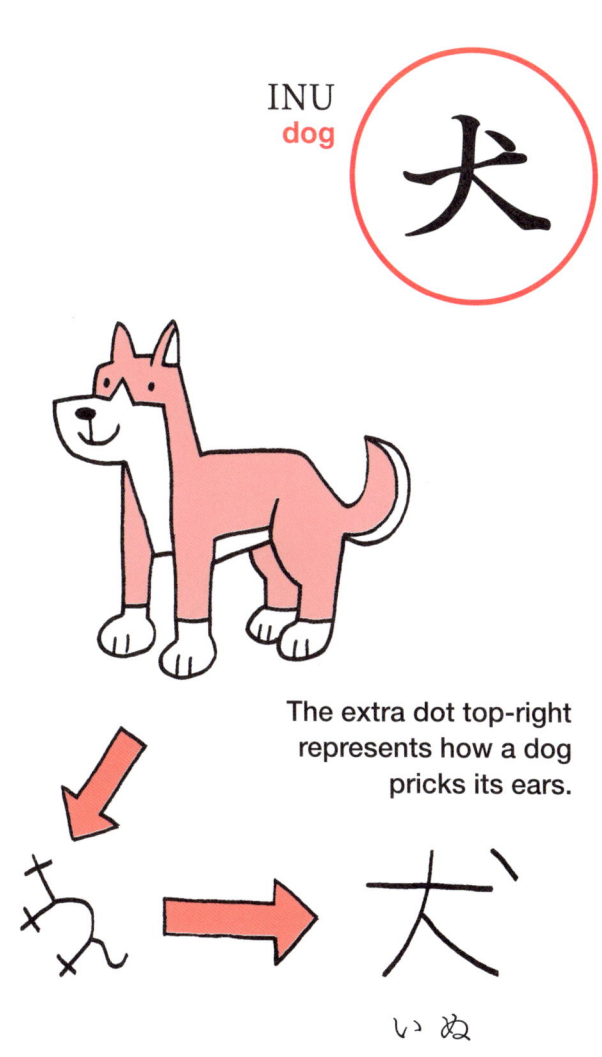

犬

The extra dot top-right represents how a dog pricks its ears.

いぬ

USHI
COW, OX

牛

A cow head. Sadly, one horn was lost when simplified.

半 ➡ 牛

うし

HITSUJI
sheep

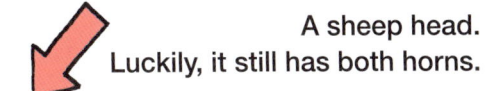

羊

A sheep head.
Luckily, it still has both horns.

ひつじ

馬

UMA
horse

A horse with four legs and a mane blowing in the wind.

馬

うま

ZOU
elephant

象

An elephant with a long snout.

象 → 象
ぞう

KAME
turtle

A simplified picture of a turtle, complete with head, shell and tail.

かめ

TORI
bird

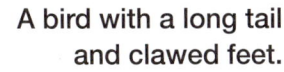

鳥

A bird with a long tail and clawed feet.

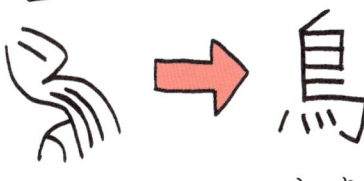

とり

41

SAKANA
fish

魚

Notice the head and body of fish were simplified the same way as turtle.

さかな

KAI
shell

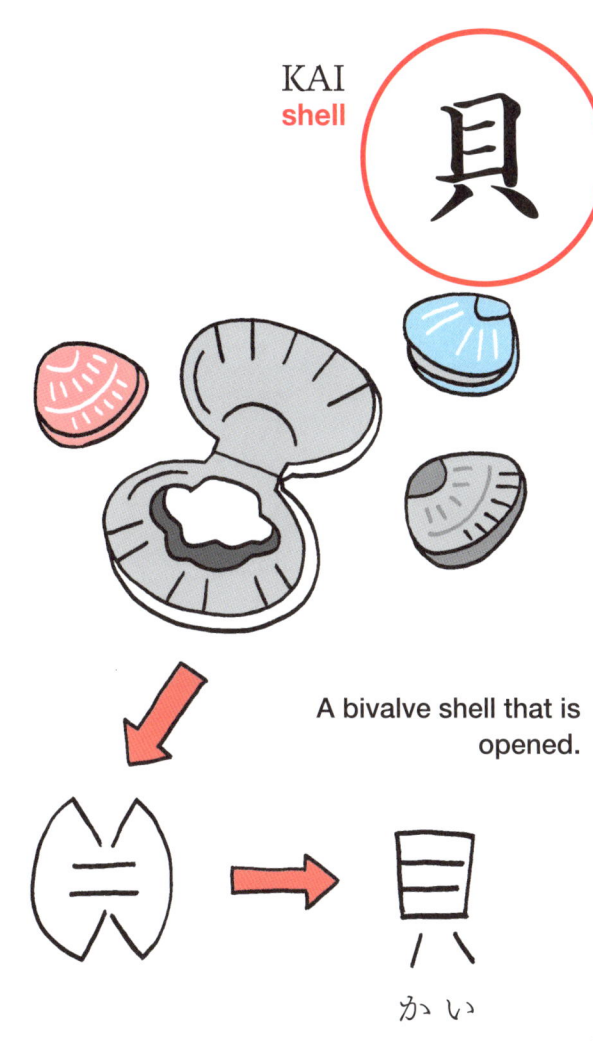

貝

A bivalve shell that is opened.

貝
かい

毛

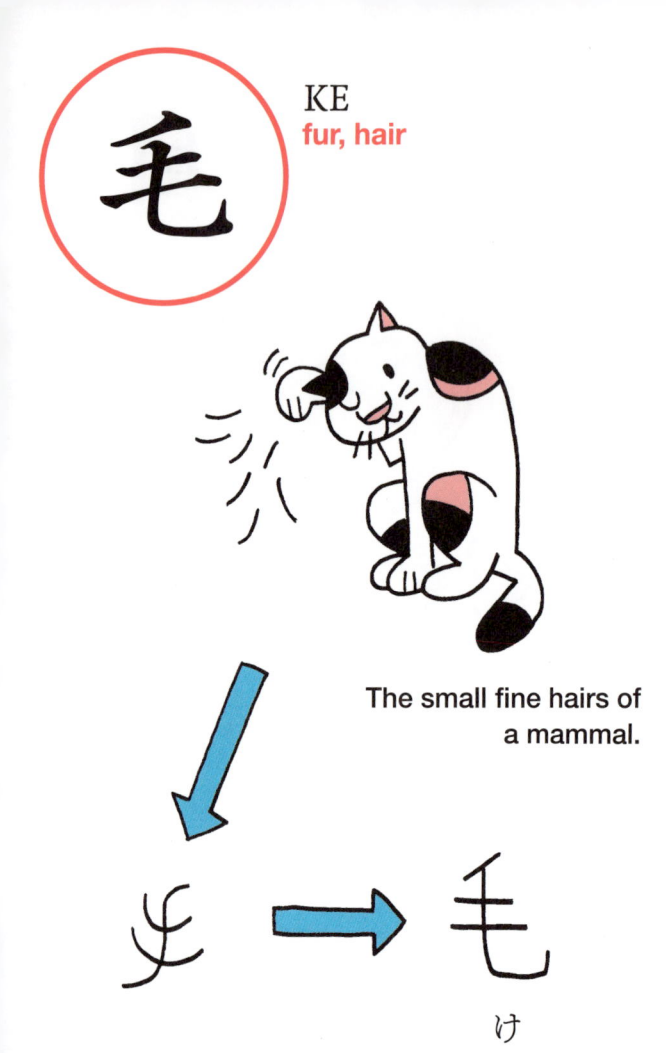

KE
fur, hair

The small fine hairs of a mammal.

け

HANE
wings

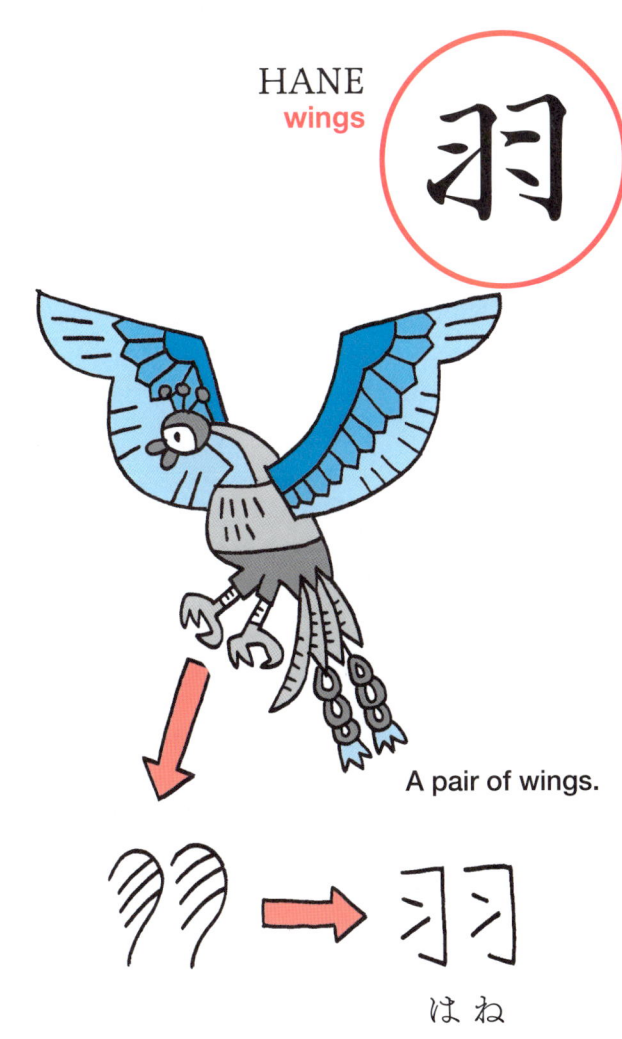

羽

A pair of wings.

羽

はね

KATANA
sword

刀

A sharp curved blade.

ノ → 刀

かたな

YAIBA, HA
blade

刃

A blade with a line marking its honed edge.

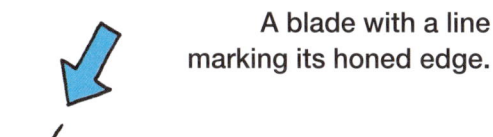

やいば

工

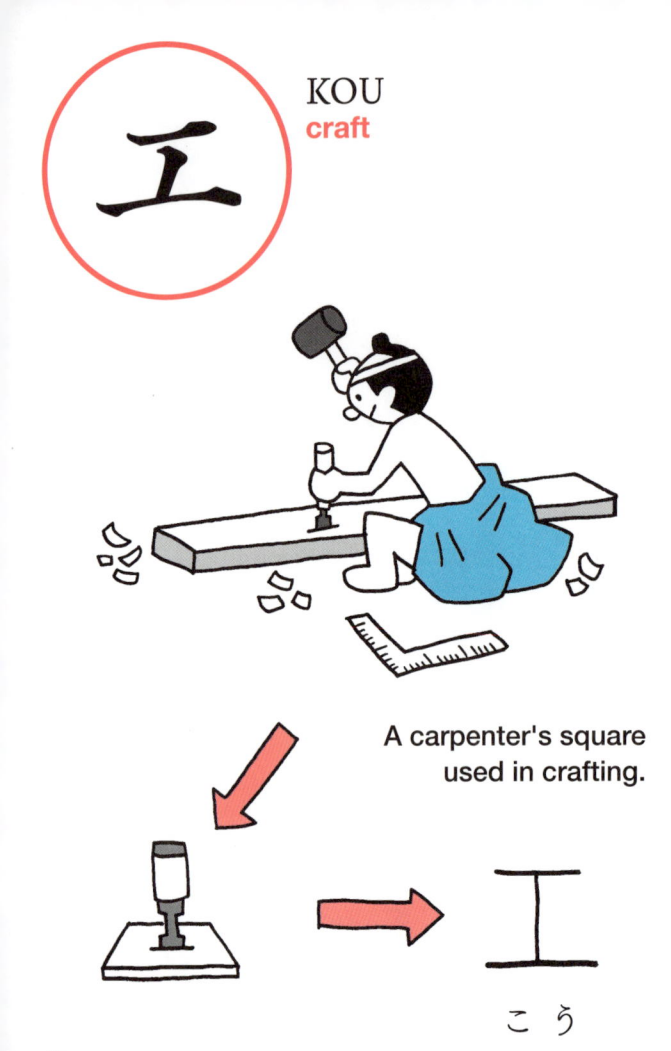

KOU
craft

A carpenter's square used in crafting.

こう

KURUMA
car

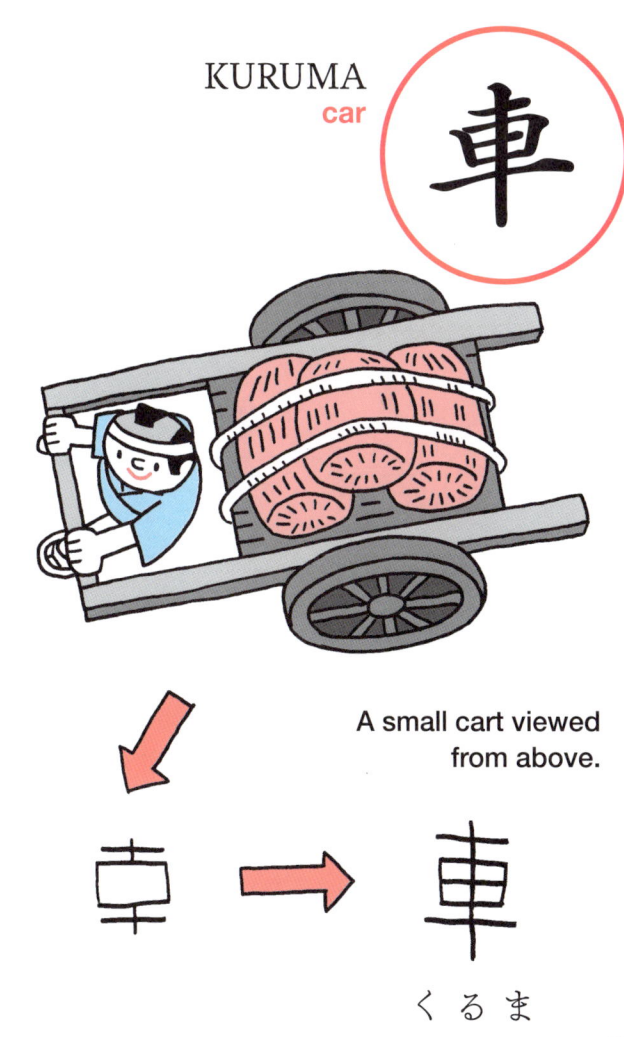

車

A small cart viewed from above.

車 → 車

くるま

FUNE
boat

舟

A small rowboat with oars and two passengers.

舟 → 舟

ふね

ITO
thread

糸

A spool of thread.

いと

YUMI
bow

A strong, flexible bow.

ゆみ

52

YA
arrow

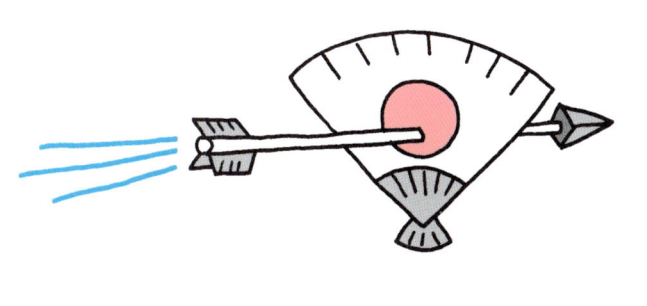

矢

A straight arrow.

や

TAMA
jewel, ball

Three jeweled beads on a string.

たま

SARA
plate

皿

A shallow dish.

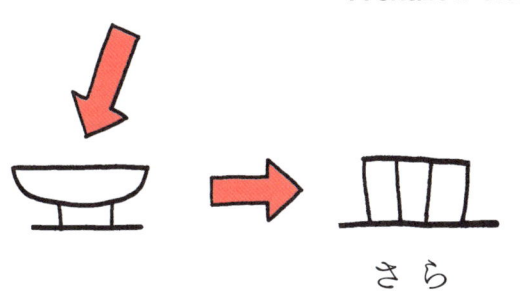

さら

井
well

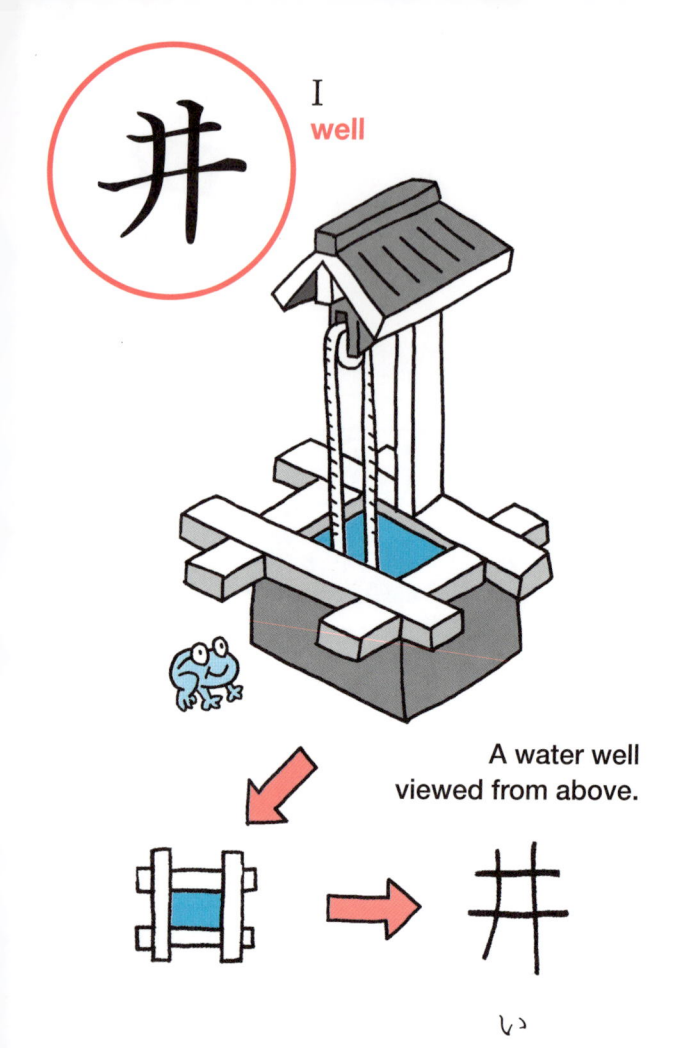

A water well viewed from above.

井

い

TO
door

戸

A swinging door
on a hinge.

と

門

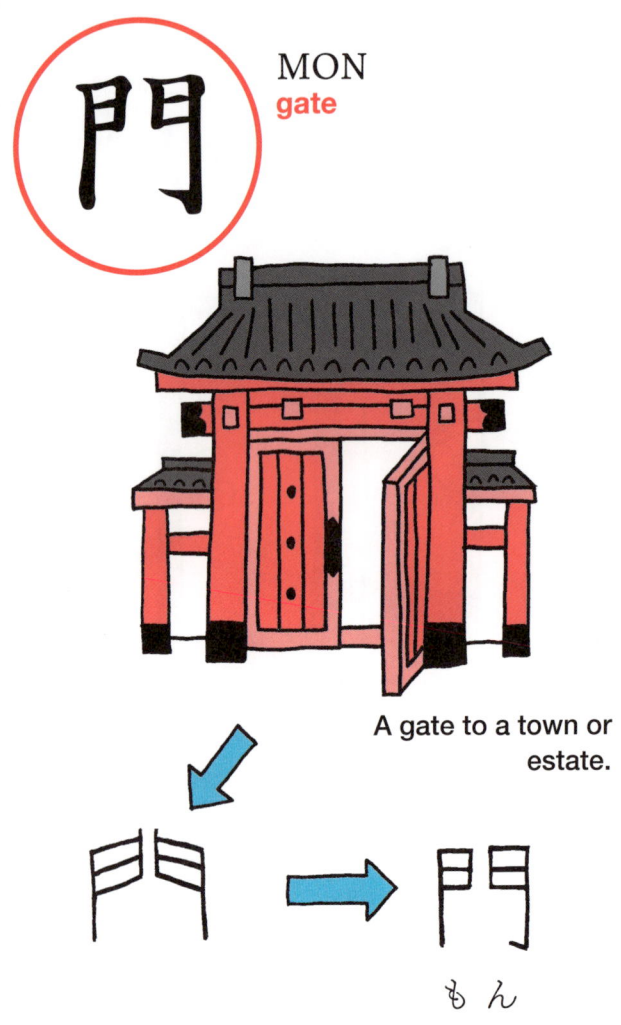

MON
gate

A gate to a town or estate.

門 → 門

もん

SATSU
volume

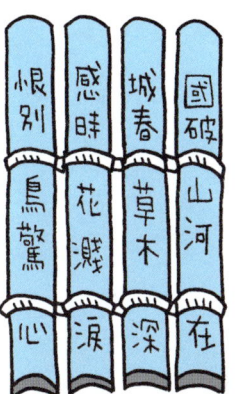

冊

Bamboo strips tied together with string collecting text into volumes.

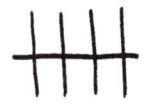

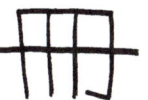

さつ

Kanji in Haiku

雪とけて
村いっぱいの子どもかな

Kanjis

雪 [yuki] snow

村 [mura] village

畑 [hatake] field

子 [ko] child

道 [michi] road

家 [ie] house

橋 [hashi] bridge

The illustration represents the scene of the following haiku.

yuki　to　ke　te
雪 と け て

mura　　　ippai　　　no
村 い っ ぱ い の

ko　do　mo　ka　na
子 ど も か な

ko bayashi　issa
小林一茶

What it means.

The snow is melting and the village is flooded with children.

The long winter ends and the snow melts at last. Now, the children of the town who have been stuck indoors can come out to play.

円

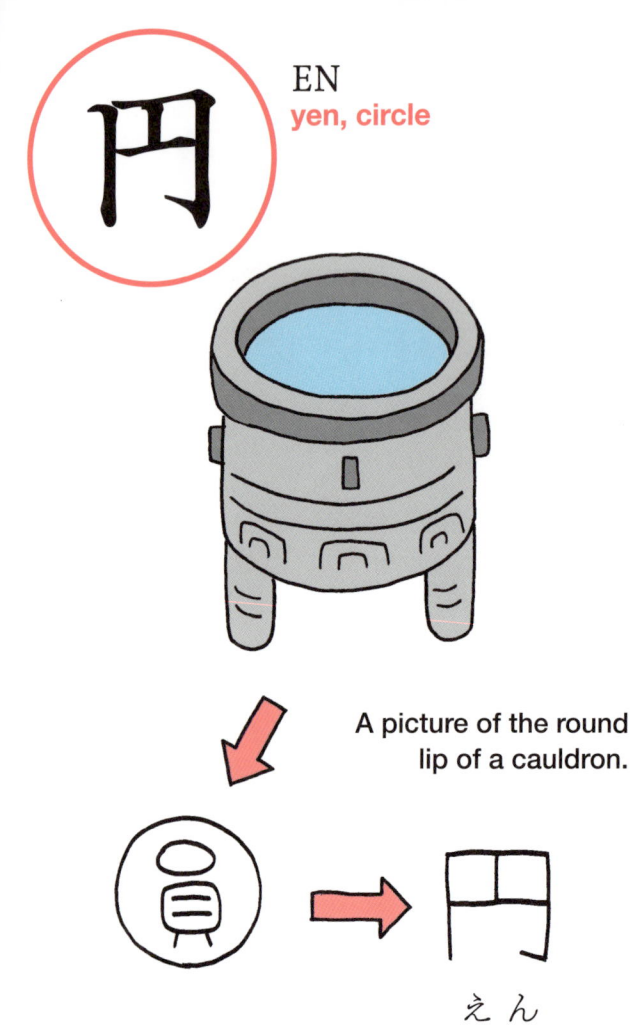

EN
yen, circle

A picture of the round lip of a cauldron.

えん

I-KU
to go, to do

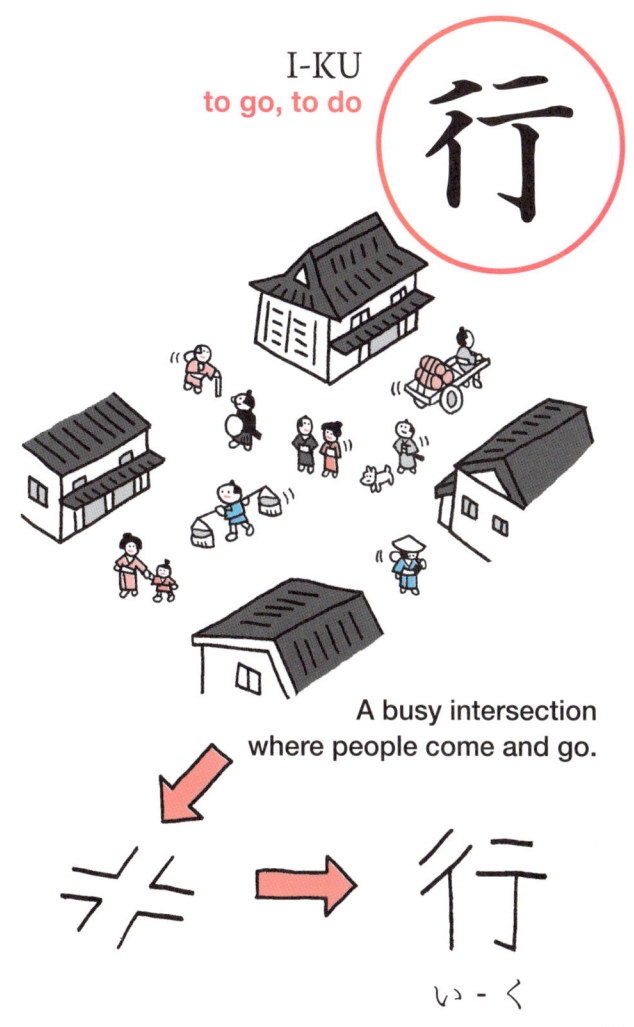

行

A busy intersection where people come and go.

い - く

KYOU
capital city

京

Roads leading up to a large building in the capital.

🡆 京

きょう

TAKA-I
high, tall, expensive

高

A tall building sitting on top a large foundation.

宫 → 高

た か - い

KOROMO
garments

The collar of a kimono drawn across the chest. The kimono is a traditional Japanese garment.

衣

ころも

KI
energy, sense

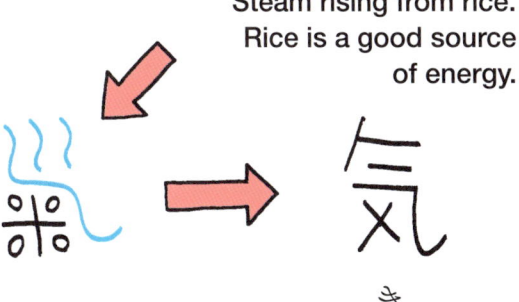

気

Steam rising from rice. Rice is a good source of energy.

き

69

回

MAWA-SU, KAI
turn, rotate, cycle

No circles allowed in kanji! So rotation here is shown using squares.

まわ-す

BUN
character, design, literature

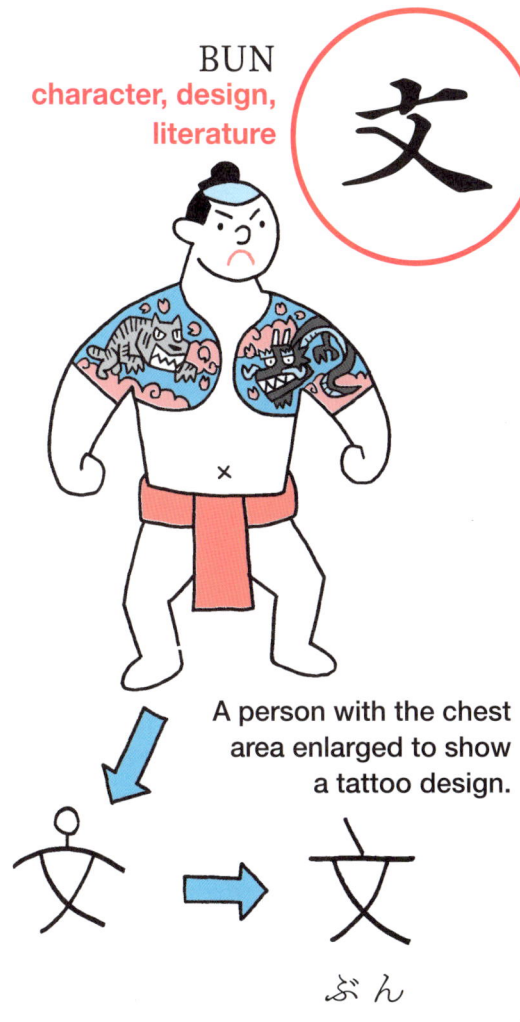

文

A person with the chest area enlarged to show a tattoo design.

ぶん

71

中

NAKA
center

A flag placed in the center of an army unit.

なか

UE
up

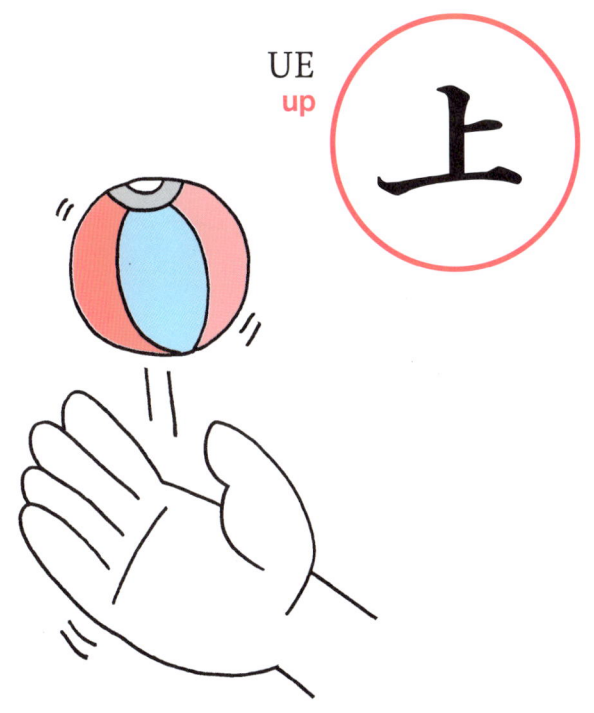

上

Throw a ball straight up.

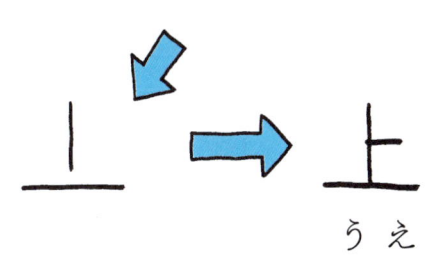

上 → 上

うえ

73

下

SHITA
down

Drop a ball straight down.

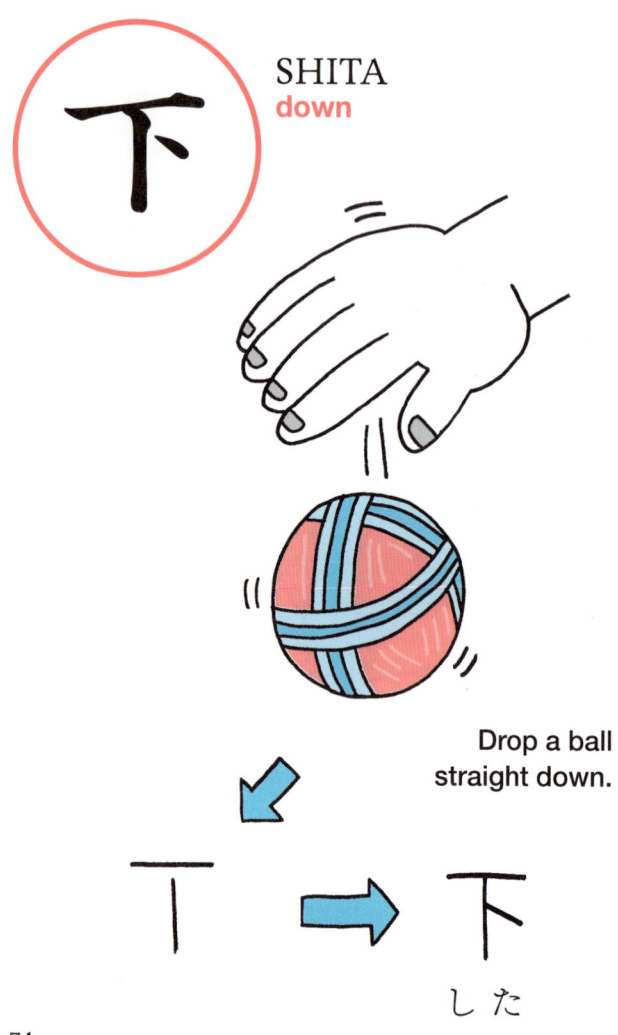

丁 ➡ 下
した

STEP2

Now we see kanji combinations and exploration of more complex concepts.

HAYASHI
woods

A line of trees make woods.

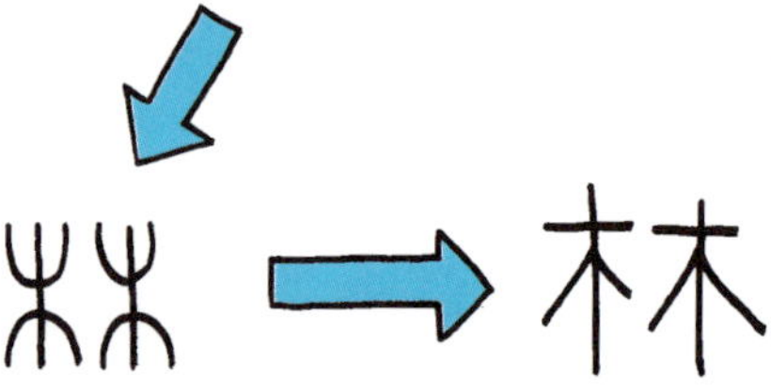

林
はやし

MORI
forest

森

Many trees make a forest.

木
森
木

もり

MOTO, HON
root, origin, book

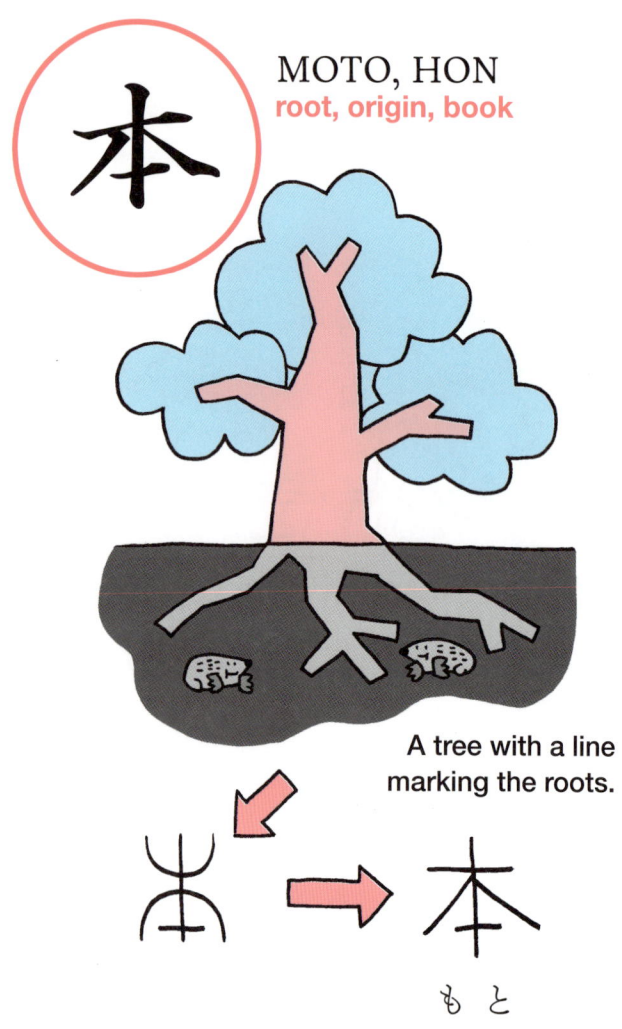

A tree with a line marking the roots.

もと

SUE, MATSU
end, terminal

末

A tree with a line marking the very end.

末 → 末

すえ

MI
not yet

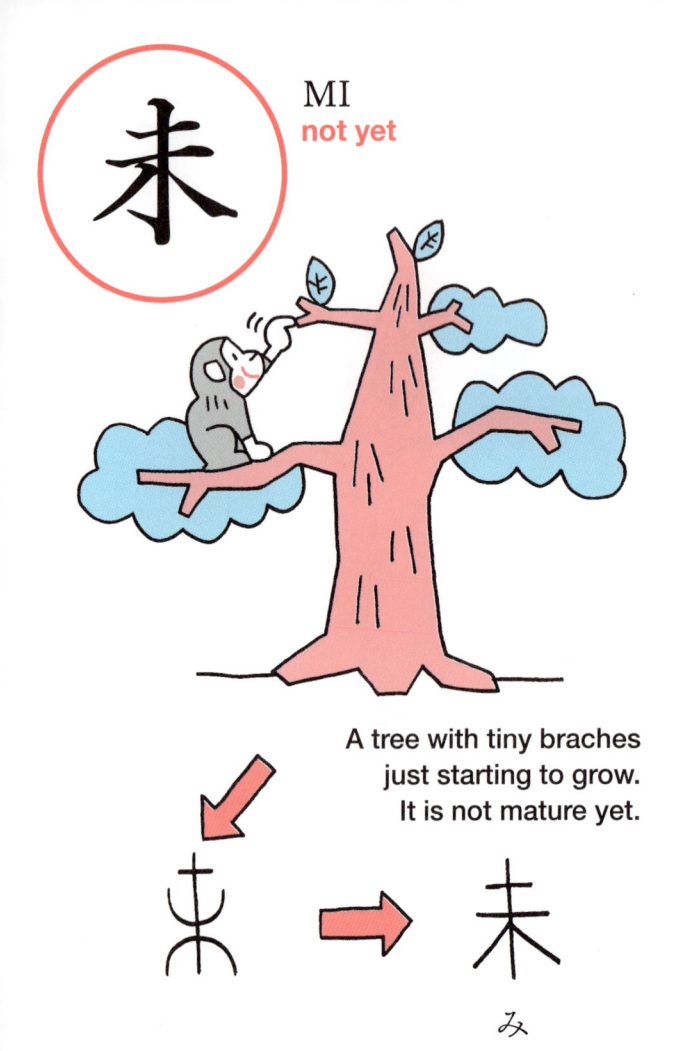

A tree with tiny braches
just starting to grow.
It is not mature yet.

み

KOMA-RU
troubled

困

A tree has trouble growing in a confined space.

こま-る

81

果

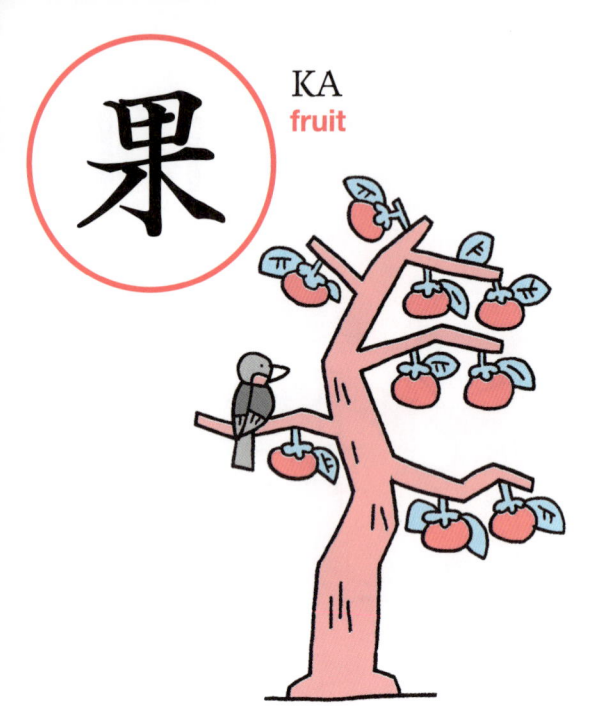

KA
fruit

A tree with ripened fruits.

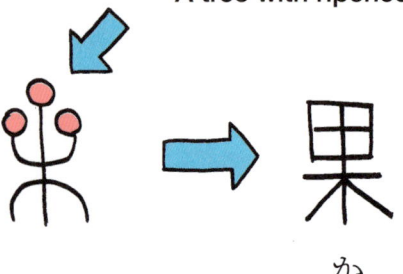

か

AKA-RUI
bright, tomorrow

明

Moonlight shining through the window brightens the room.

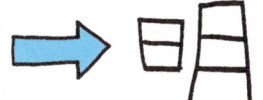

◉)) → 明

あか‐るい

YUU
evening

夕

A crescent moon, barely visible in the sky as evening sets in.

ゆう

U-MARERU, I-KIRU
life, birth, grow

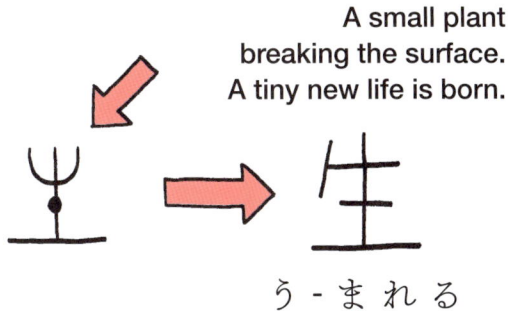

生

A small plant breaking the surface.
A tiny new life is born.

う-まれる

HOSHI
star

星

Stars look like little suns starting to sprout and grow.

星
ほし

HONOO
flame

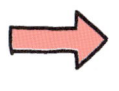

炎

A fiery flame rising high.

炎

ほのお

WAZAWA-I
disaster

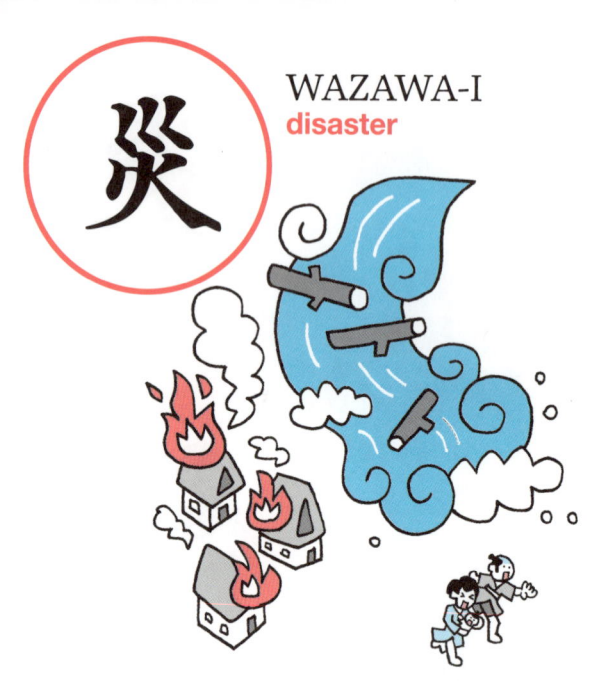

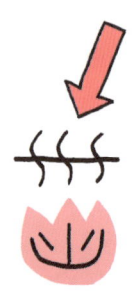

Even in modern-day Japan, disaster can strike in the form of raging fires and flooding rivers.

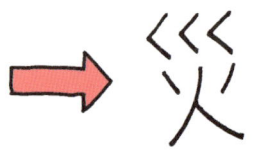

わざわ-い

HIKARI
light, shine

光

A flame carried above a person's head, shining in all directions.

ひかり

KOME
rice

A fully-grown rice stalk ready for harvest.

こめ

TAKE
bamboo

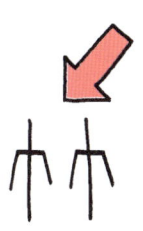

竹

Two bamboo trees with branches on either side.

たけ

Kanji in Haiku

花散るや
耳ふって馬の
おとなしさ

Kanji

桜 [sakura] cherry blossom

散 [chi-ru] scatter

耳 [mimi] ear

杭 [kui] post

馬 [uma] horse

綱 [tsuna] rope

虫 [mushi] bug

The illustration represents the scene of the following haiku.

はな ちる や
花 散 る や

みみ ふって うま の
耳 ふ っ て 馬 の

お と な し さ
お と な し さ

むらかみ き じょう
村 上 鬼 城

What it means.

Cherry blossoms fall
and scatter around a horse
his ears move gently

A horse grazes under a cherry blossom tree and gently flicks its ears as falling petals flutter about. A peaceful scene of springtime coming to an end.

早

HAYA-I
early, quick

Early morning, when the sun begins to rise overhead.

はや-い

OO-KII
big, large

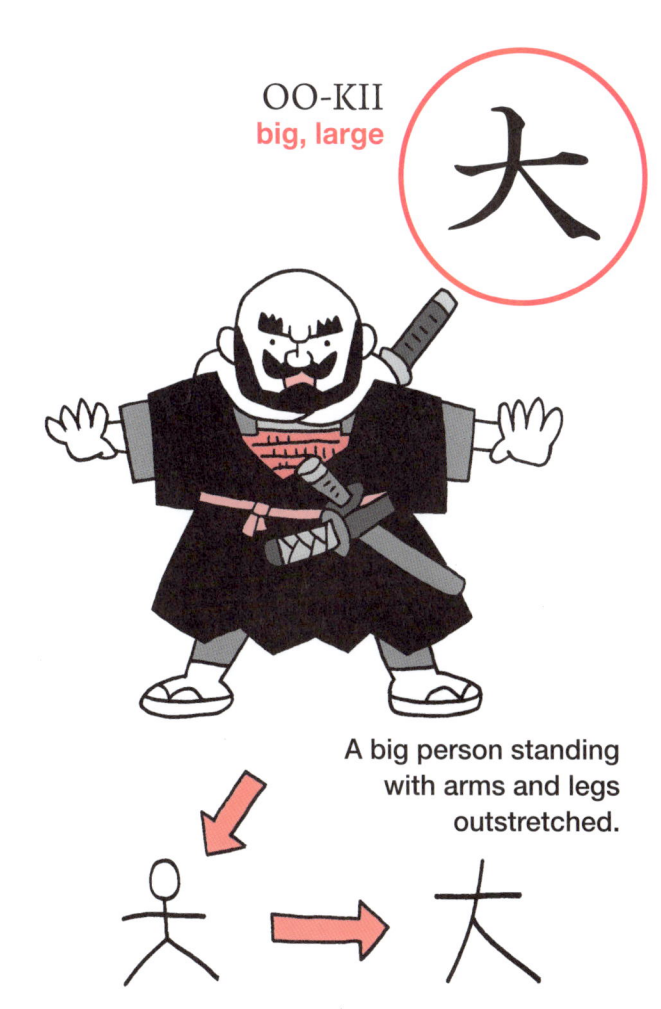

大

A big person standing with arms and legs outstretched.

大 → 大

おお-きい

TEN
the sky, the heavens

A person with a line representing the sky stretching far and wide overhead.

てん

TA-TSU
stand

立

A person standing in place with a line to show the ground.

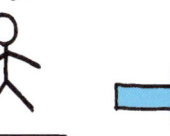

た - つ

化

BA-KERU
change, transform

Two people, one standing upright and one flipped upside-down. This woman transformed into a cat!

ば - け る

KURA-BERU
compare

比

Two people standing one behind the other. These men compare today's catch.

比 → 比

くら-べる

101

SHITA
tongue

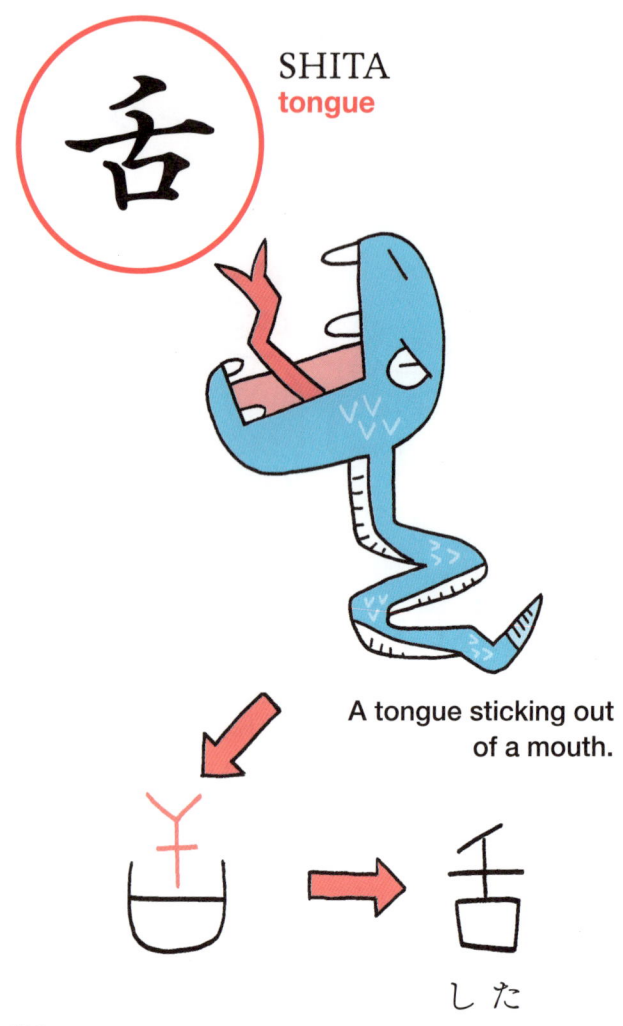

A tongue sticking out of a mouth.

した

102

HIN
goods, product

品

Several boxes piled together. They are goods to be delivered.

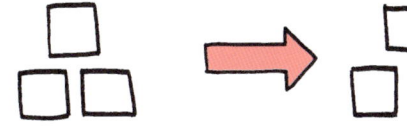

しな

NA
name

名

A crescent moon and mouth. People would call out to ask someone's name when it was too dark to see.

な

FU-KU
blow

吹

A person facing left with their mouth open and blowing on something.

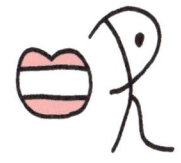

ふ - く

言

I-U
say, speak

臨兵闘者
皆陳列在前

Open the mouth and move the tongue to speak words. He is performing a ninja chant.

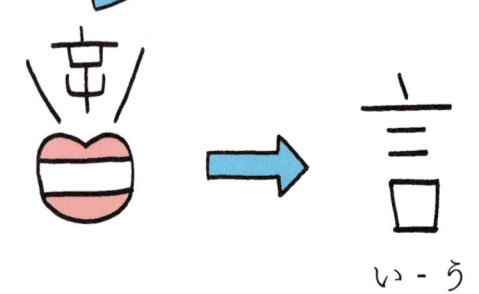

い-う

HANA-SU
talk

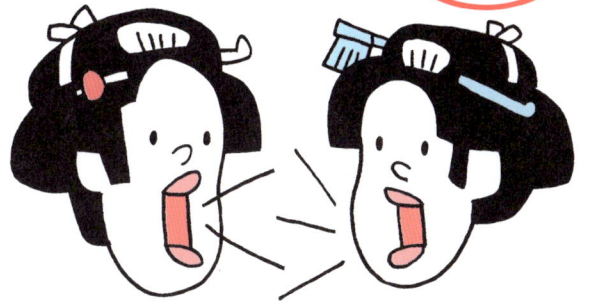

話

This kanji emphasizes use of the tongue to talk eloquently and at length.

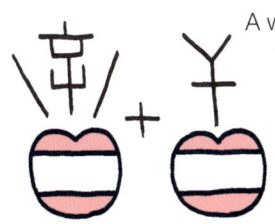

A wagging tongue.

→ 話

はな-す

音

OTO
sound

A person with their mouth covered cannot speak, but only makes sound.

音

おと

UTA
song, sing

歌

A person with their mouth open wide to sing a song.

歌
うた

右

MIGI
right

A right hand holding an item.

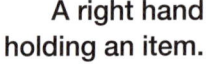

右
みぎ

HIDARI
left

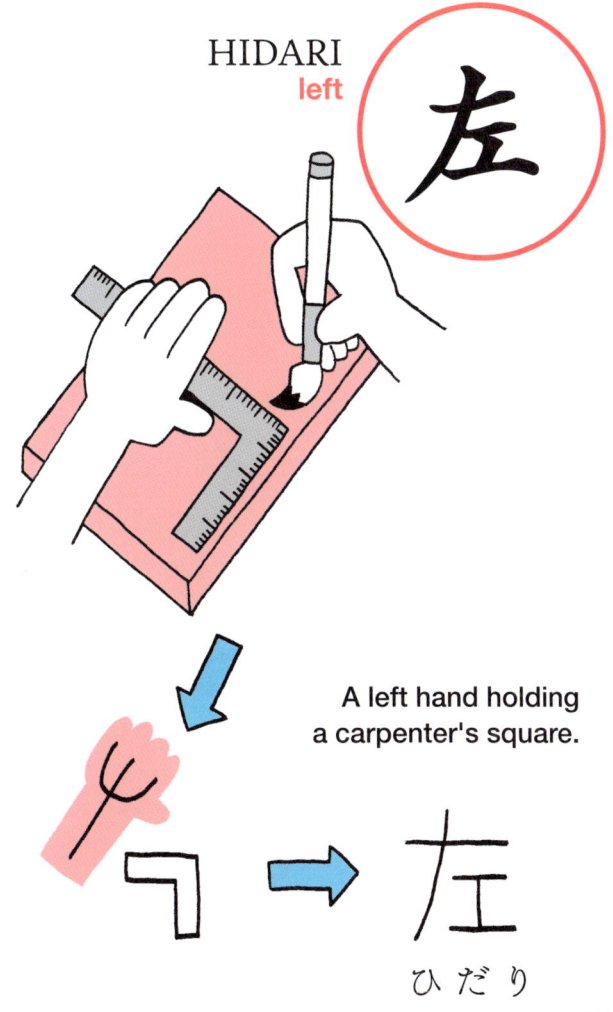

左

A left hand holding a carpenter's square.

ヲ → 左

ひだり

友

TOMO
friend

Two bros locking hands in eternal friendship.

→ 友
とも

112

TOMO
together

共

Two hands working together to lift up.

共
とも

113

ARASO-U
quarrel

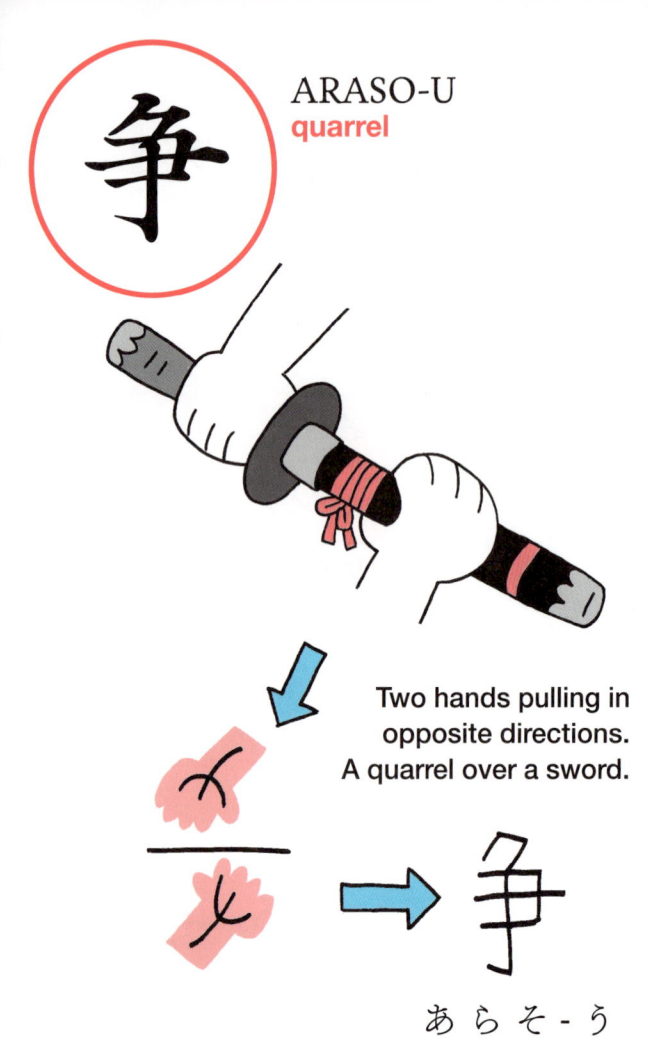

Two hands pulling in opposite directions. A quarrel over a sword.

あらそ-う

KOBUSHI
fist

拳

A firmly clenched fist.

拳

こぶし

止

TO-MERU
stop

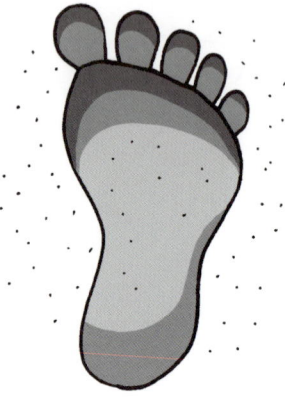

A footprint, indicating a foot stopped in place.

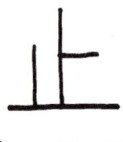

と - める

HASHI-RU
run

走

A person running with arms outstreched with a footprint underneath.

走

はし-る

歩

ARU-KU
walk

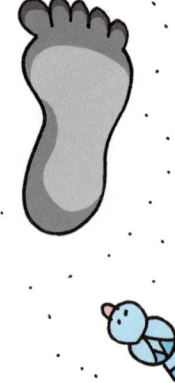

Two footprints in succession.
Walk on the sand and
leave your footprints.

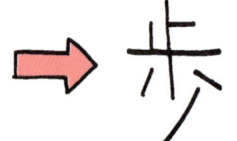

→ 歩

ある-く

TADA-SHII
correct

正

A footprint with a line above it. Right here–this is the correct place to be.

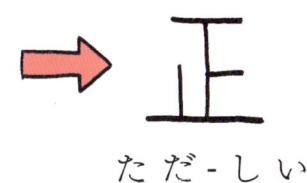

→ 正

ただ-しい

119

出

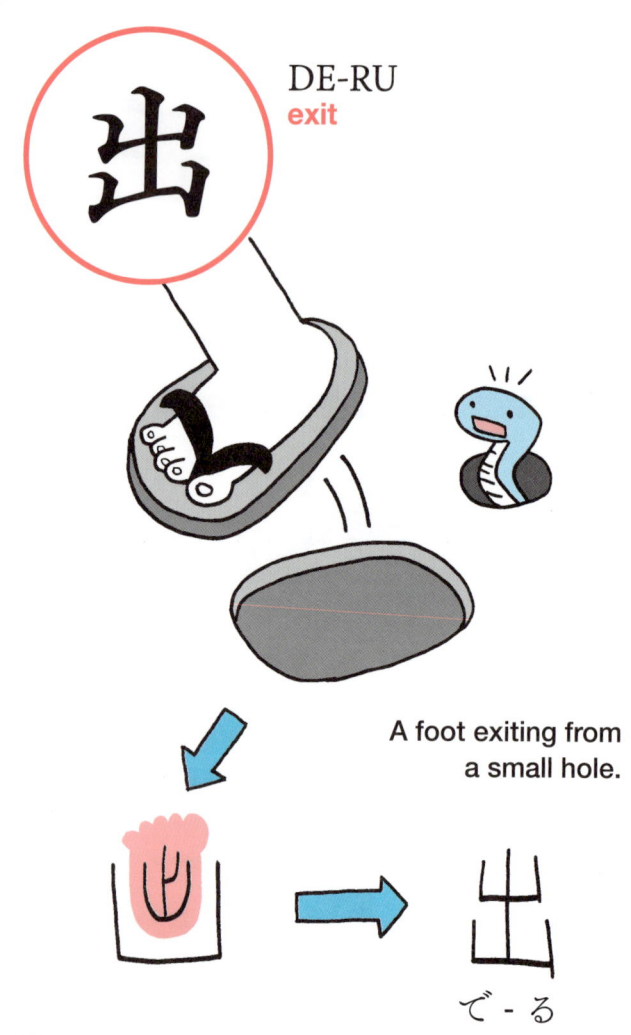

DE-RU
exit

A foot exiting from a small hole.

で-る

MI-RU
see

見

A person with the eye drawn large for emphasis.

み - る

121

Kanji in Haiku

柿くへば
鐘が鳴るなり
法隆寺

Kanji

空 [sora] sky

雲 [kumo] cloud

柿 [kaki] persimmon

鐘 [kane] bell

塔 [tou] tower

寺 [tera] temple

**The illustration represents
the scene of the following haiku.**

kaki ku e ba
柿 く へ ば

kane ga na ru na ri
鐘 が 鳴 る な り

ho ryu ji
法 隆 寺

masa oka shi ki
正 岡 子 規

What it means.

Eating a persimmon and the bell tolls at Horyuji Temple

Shiki was eating persimmon at a tea shop in Horyuji Temple when the bell began to toll. Images of Horyuji Temple — the oldest wooden building in the world — along with persimmons and the solemn toll of the bell are strongly associated with autumn.

覚

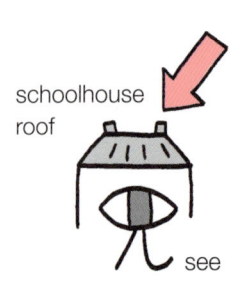

OBO-ERU
remember

schoolhouse roof — see

Remember what you see and hear at school.

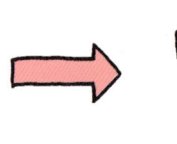

覚

おぼ-える

SAKI
before, ahead

先

A person who has started before and has progressed farther than you, leaving their footprints.

→ 先
さき

休

YASU-MU
rest

A person taking a rest against a tree.

や す-む

NA-KUNARU
disappear, die

亡

A screen hides a woman so she disappears from view.

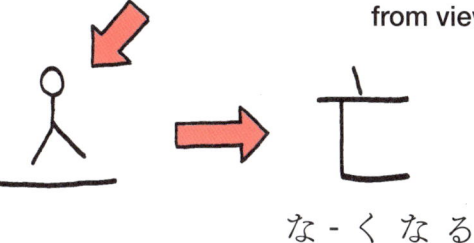

な-くなる

考

KANGA-ERU
think

Just think of an old man hunched over in thought. Or is he just sleeping…?

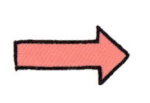

かんが-える

TSUTSU-MU
wrap

包

Japanese wrap gifts in cloth called "furoshiki."

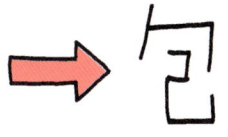

→ 包

つつ-む

131

NAGA-I
long

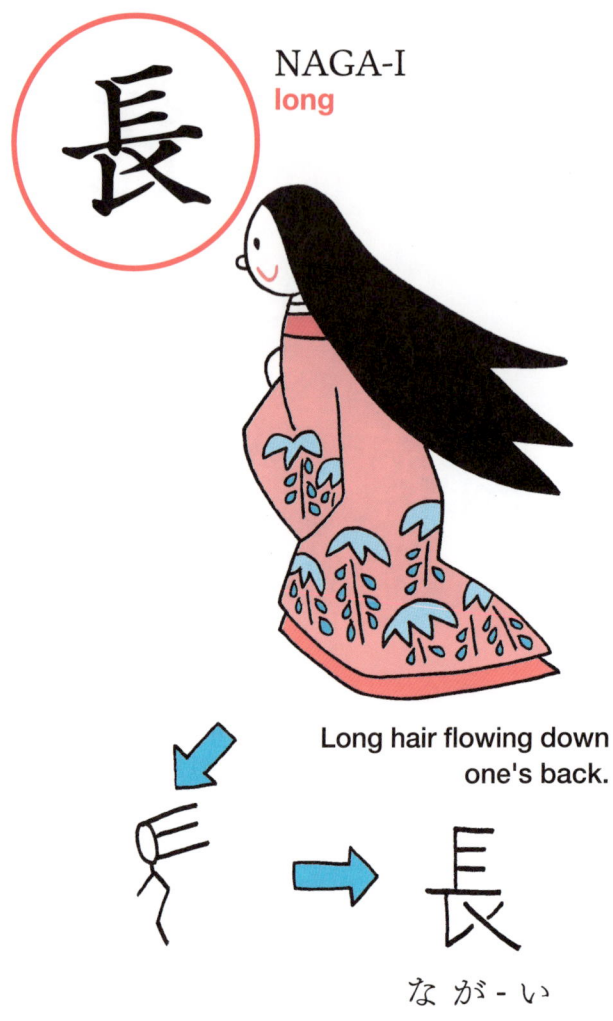

Long hair flowing down one's back.

長
な が - い

132

ONI
ogre, demon

鬼

A creature with a large scary face and a horn on its head. A will-o-wisp follows him.

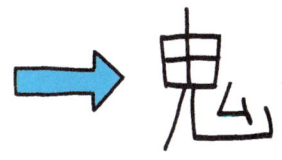

おに

133

背

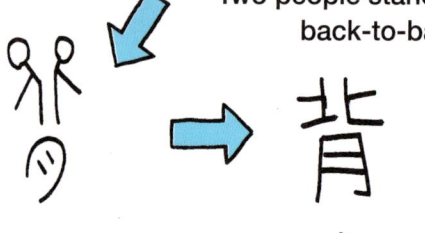

SE
back

Two people standing back-to-back.

せ

MEN
mask, face

面

A mask that hides everything but the eyes.

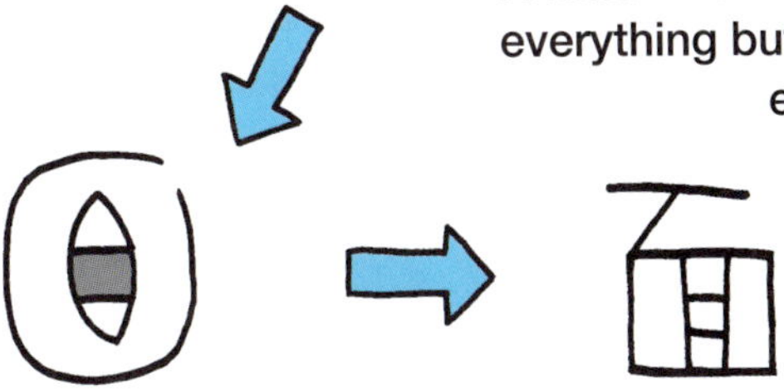

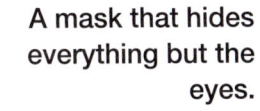

めん

135

取

TO-RU
take

Warriors would take the ears of their enemies as spoils during battle.

耳 + 又 → 取

と - る

HAJI
embarrassment, shame

恥

When embarrassed, the heart pumps blood furiously, and the ears turn red.

→ 恥

はじ

劣

OTO-RU
inferior

little 少 + 力 → 劣
おと-る

Having little power makes you inferior to your opponent.

KYOU
cooperation

協

Cooperation is the intersection of everyone's strength.

きょう

139

FURU-I
old

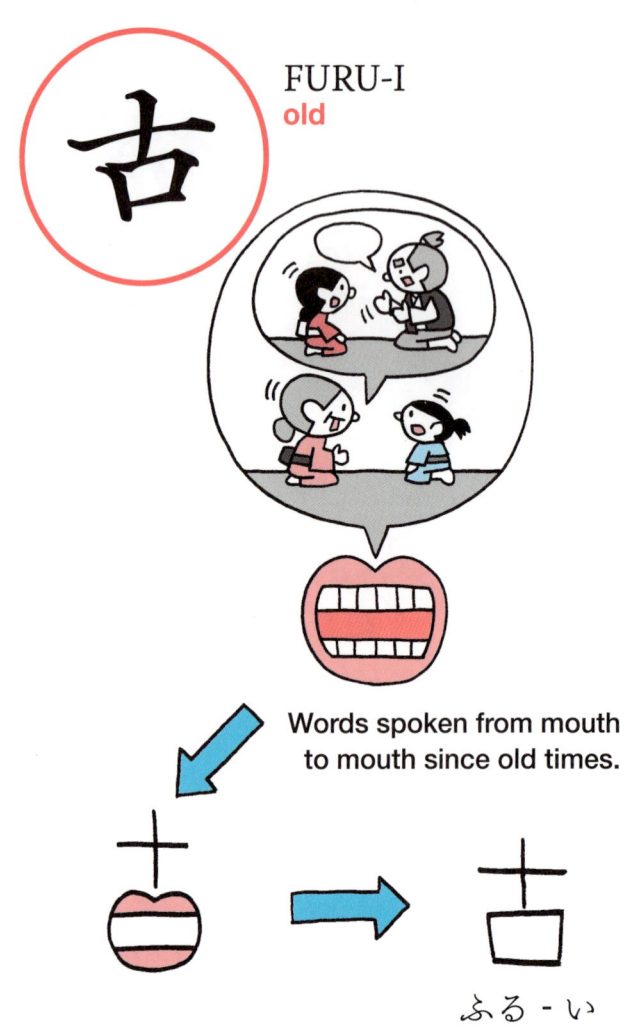

Words spoken from mouth to mouth since old times.

ふる-い

SHI
death

死

Crumbled bones and a person crumpled over combine to represent death.

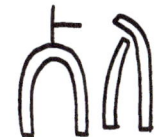

死
し

MACHI
town

Sections of land with clear divisions made to indicate town limits.

田 + 亅 ➡ 町

まち

142

OTOKO
man

男

A man uses his strength to work in the rice field.

おとこ

A-TARU
strike, win

Hit the jackpot and money falls into your hand.

あ - た る

144

STEP3

Having fun yet?
Let's look at some
more kanji!

WA
harmony

Rice stalks bending with the wind and mouths represent voices in harmony and agreement.

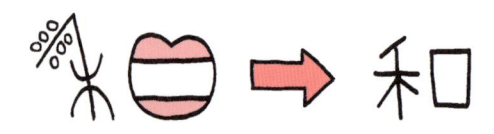

わ

HANA
flower

花

Flowers are plants that change from bud to blossom.

plants

change

→ 花

はな

147

苦

KURU-SHII, NIGA-I
suffer, bitter

Old plants taste bitter.

old → 苦

くる-しい

KUSA
grass

草

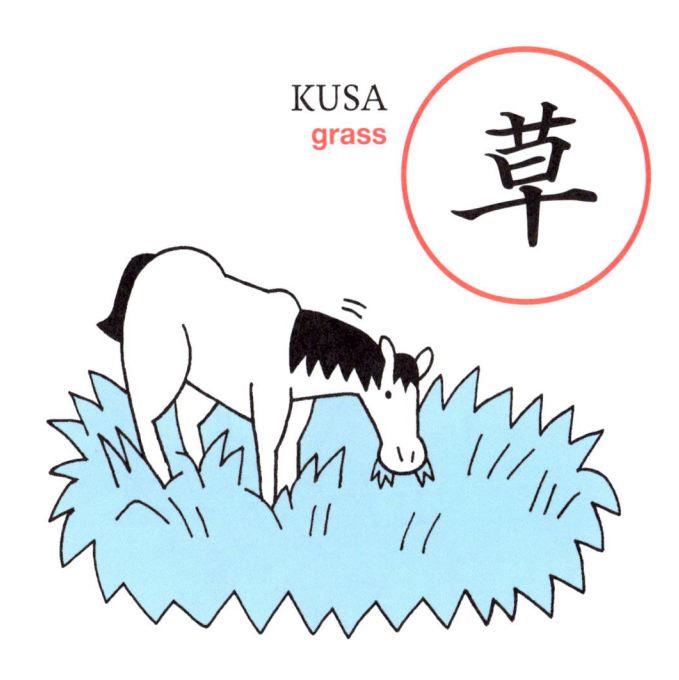

A general term for grass. It's too early to tell what will grow here.

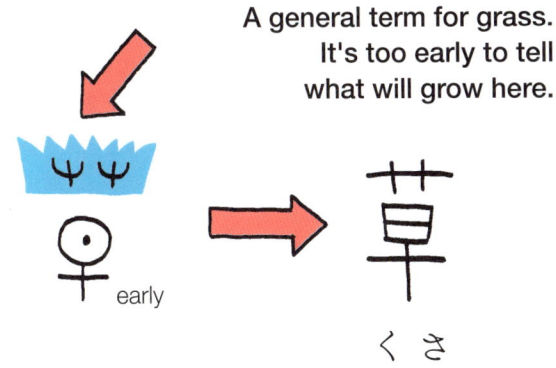

early → 草
くさ

149

小

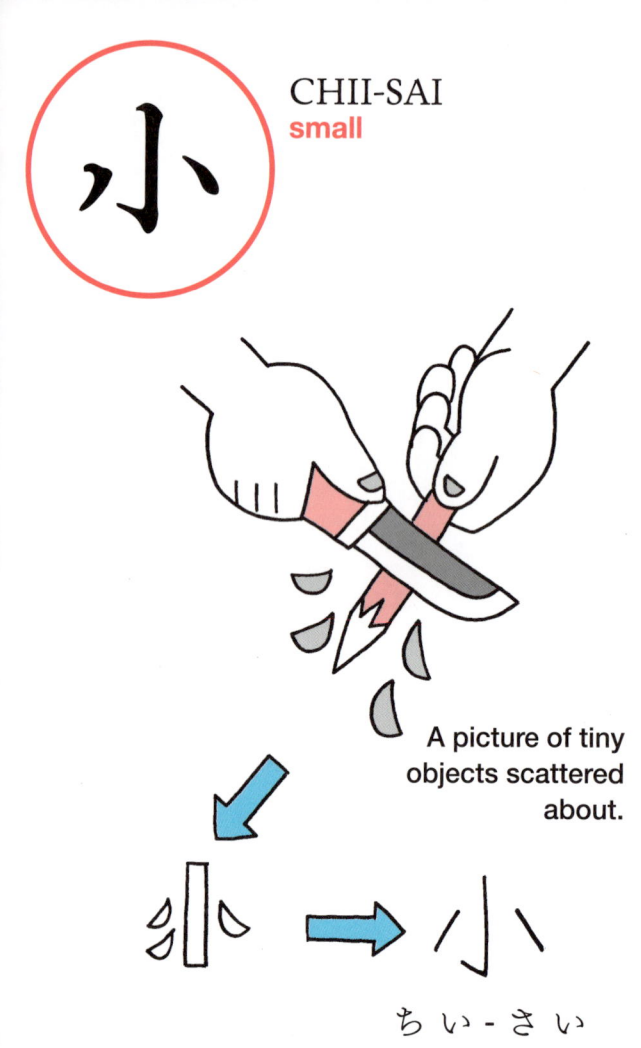

CHII-SAI
small

A picture of tiny objects scattered about.

ち い - さ い

HAN
half

半

Splitting a cow in half to prepare it for sacrifice. He seems fine with it.

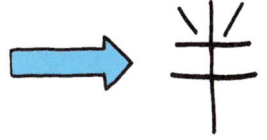

はん

TO-BU
fly, jump

飛

A picture of two birds flying.

とぶ

ATSU-MARU
gather

集

Birds gathered in a tree.

集

あつ-まる

Kanji in Haiku

酒もすき
餅もすきなり
今朝の春

Kanji

夫 [otto] husband

妻 [tsuma] wife

餅 [mochi] rice cake

箸 [hashi] chopsticks

酒 [sake] sake

猫 [neko] cat

The illustration represents the scene of the following haiku.

_{sake mo su ki}
酒もすき

_{mochi mo su ki na ri}
餅もすきなり

_{kesa no haru}
今朝の春

_{taka hama kyo shi}
高浜虚子

What it means.

I like sake
I also like rice cake -
On this New Year's morning

On New Year's, people drink sake and eat rice cake. This poem is Kyoshi enjoying his favorite food and drink to ring in the new year, called "oshogatsu."

鳴

NA-RU, NA-KU
cry, call

A combination of mouth and bird, this character represents animal calls and alarm sounds.

口 + 鳥 → 鳴

な - る

UTSUKU-SHII
beautiful

美

A large sheep has a beautiful coat of wool and provides delicious meat.

うつく-しい

159

KUSA-I
smelly

Dogs are known for their keen sense of smell.

臭
く さ - い

SUSU-MU
progress

進

Progressing smoothly like a bird through the sky.

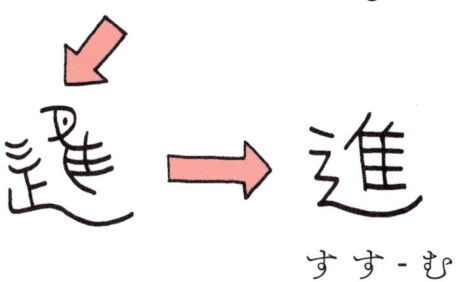

進 → 進

すす-む

161

KOORI
ice

氷

Cracks in the surface of ice.
You can see water through
cracks in the ice.

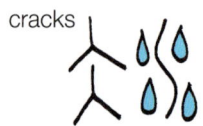

cracks → 氷

こおり

162

SU-KI
like 好

A picture of a woman with her beloved child.

好 → 好

す - き

泡

AWA
bubble

A watery film wrapped into a bubble shape.

あわ

YUKI
snow

雪

Snow is rain you can hold in your hand.

雪
ゆき

DEN
electricity

A combination of rain and lightning, this kanji is now mostly used to reference electricity.

でん

YASU-I
inexpensive, safe

安

Taking a wife and bringing a woman under your roof makes for a calmer, more stable household.

やす-い

MAI
every

Every person has a mother.

まい

HAI-RU
enter

入

The entrance to a tent.

は い - る

穴

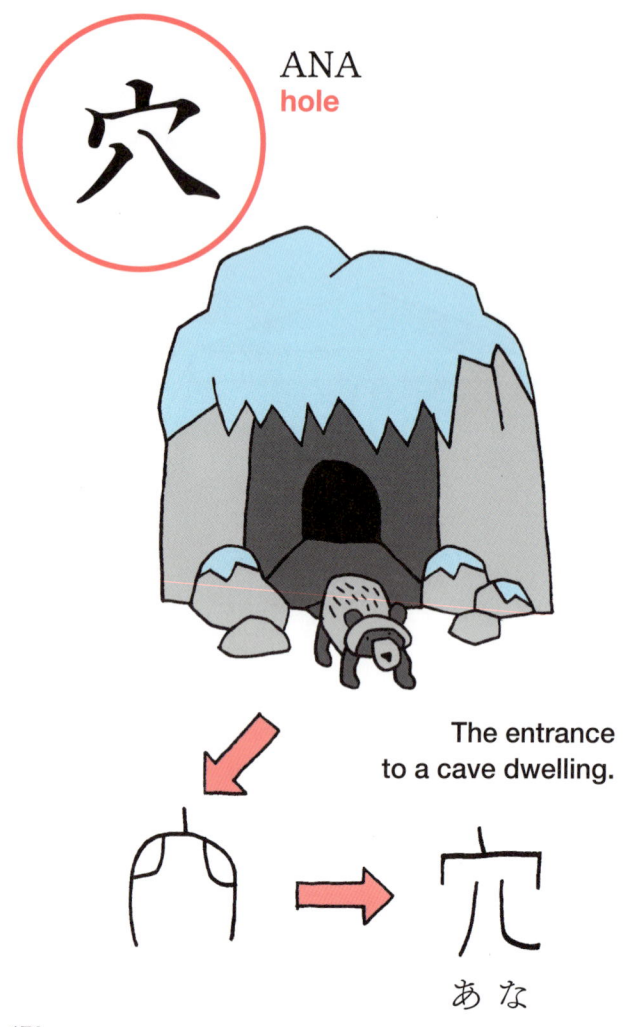

ANA
hole

The entrance to a cave dwelling.

あな

MANA-BU
learn

学

school house roof

child

Children learn many things at school.

学 → 学

まな-ぶ

SHIME-SU
show

示

A picture of an altar. People made sacrifices and hoped the gods would show themselves in the form of a sign.

示 ➡ 示

しめ-す

BUN
part, minute

分

Using a sword to split something into parts. Used to represent minutes and fractions.

分 → 分
ぶん

切

KI-RU
cut

Cut something with a sword. The left side is a slash mark.

十り → 切

き - る

HI-KU
pull

引

Pull the string of a bow taut.

引 → 引

ひ - く

合

A-U
match

A lid on top of a container. The lid matches the container.

あ - う

会

A-U
meet

A lid on top of a steaming pot of stew. Meet a friend and dine together.

あ - う

ONA-JI
same

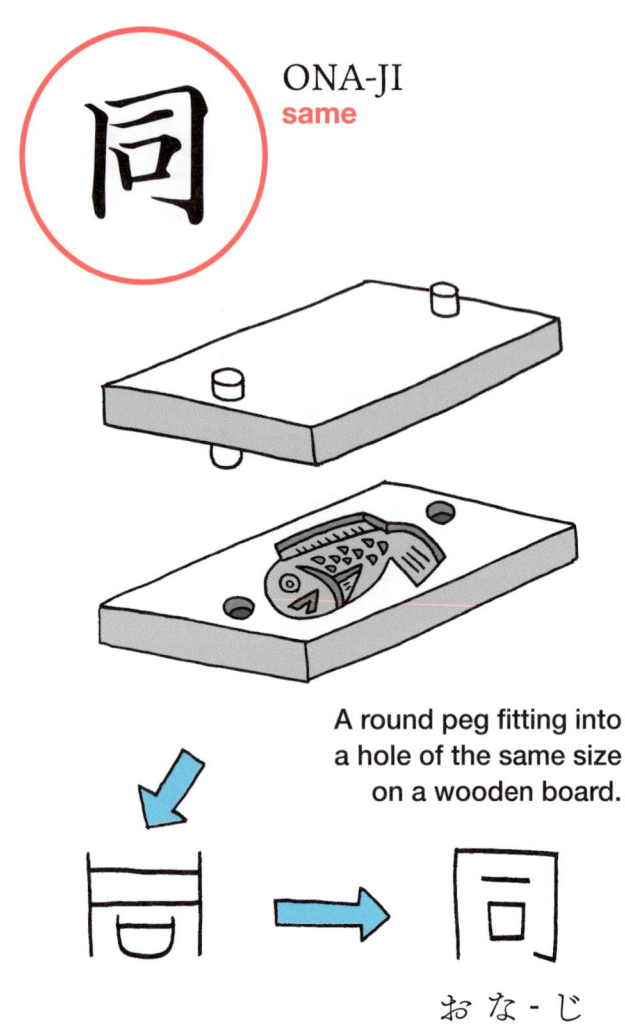

同

A round peg fitting into a hole of the same size on a wooden board.

お な - じ

GU
tool

具

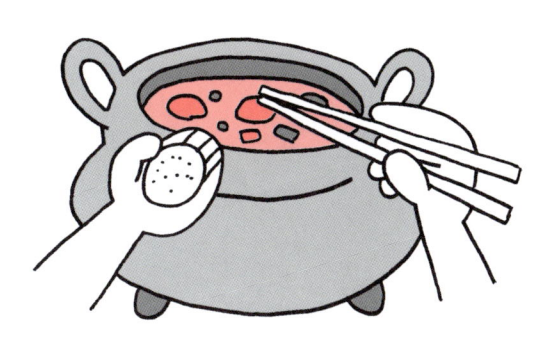

Two hands using a cauldron to prepare food.

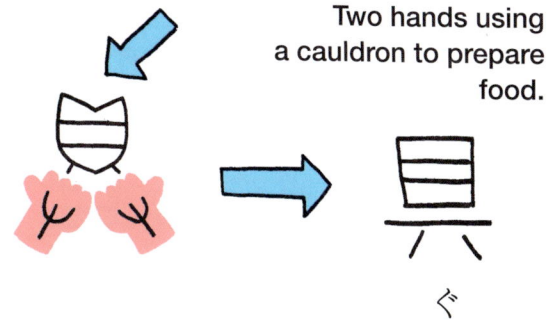

具

ぐ

重

OMO-I
heavy

A person carrying a heavy bundle of stuff and things.

おも-い

U-KERU
receive

受

One hand passing an item to another hand.

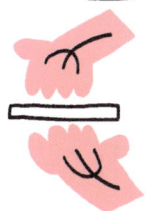

受

う - ける

TA-BERU
eat

A bowl of white rice with a lid. Just needs a little soy sauce…

た - べ る

NO-MU
drink

飲

A person with their mouth open sipping tea.

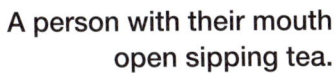

食 + 欠 → 飲

の - む

183

Kanji in Haiku

赤い椿白い椿と落ちにけり

Kanji

赤 [aka] red

白 [shiro] white

椿 [tsubaki] camellia

落 [o-tiru] fall

The illustration represents the scene of the following haiku.

<small>aka　　i　　tsubaki</small>
赤 い 椿

<small>shiro　i　　tsubaki　to</small>
白 い 椿 と

<small>o　　chi　　ni　　ke　　ri</small>
落 ち に け り

<small>kawa higashi heki　go　　dou</small>
河 東 碧 梧 桐

What it means.

Red camellia
then white camellia
falling down

Camellia blossoms are falling; red followed by white. Despite being quite vibrant already, the contrast in color makes each one appear all the more vivid.

多

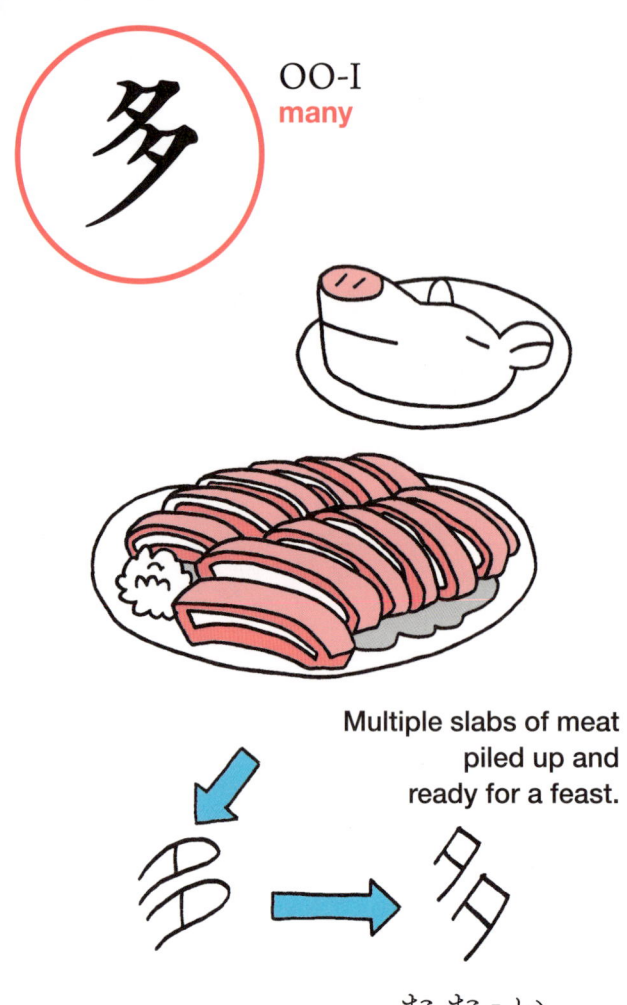

OO-I
many

Multiple slabs of meat piled up and ready for a feast.

おお-い

TSU-KU
attach

付

A hand reaching to place something on a person.

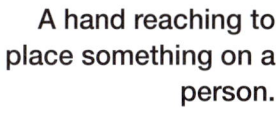

付
つ-く

189

仲

NAKA
relationship

The relationship that exists between two people.

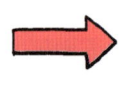

なか

KARADA
body

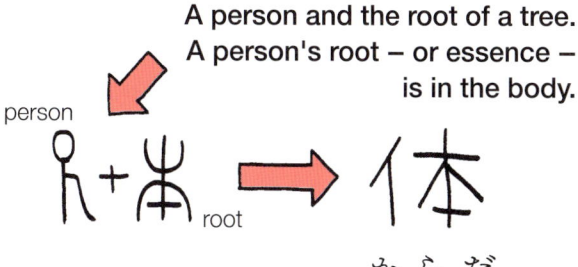

体

A person and the root of a tree.
A person's root – or essence –
is in the body.

person → 𠇖 + 本 root ⇒ 体
からだ

保

TAMO-TSU
save, preserve

This kanji depicts a parent giving their child a piggyback.

たも-つ

192

TO-U
ask

問

Call out at the front gate
to ask permission to enter.

と - う

193

聞

KI-KU
hear

Put your ear to the gate to hear what's inside.

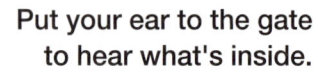

き - く

NA-GERU
throw

投

A picture of a hand holding a stick. The hand element indicates motion of the hand.

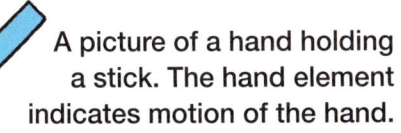

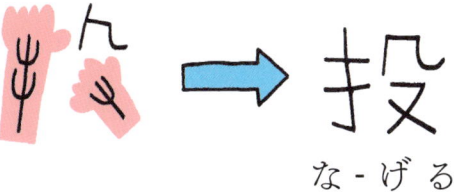

な-げる

抱

DA-KU
hug

Wrap your arms around someone to give them a hug.

扌 + 包 → 抱
だ - く

SHINO-BU, NIN
bear, hide, endure

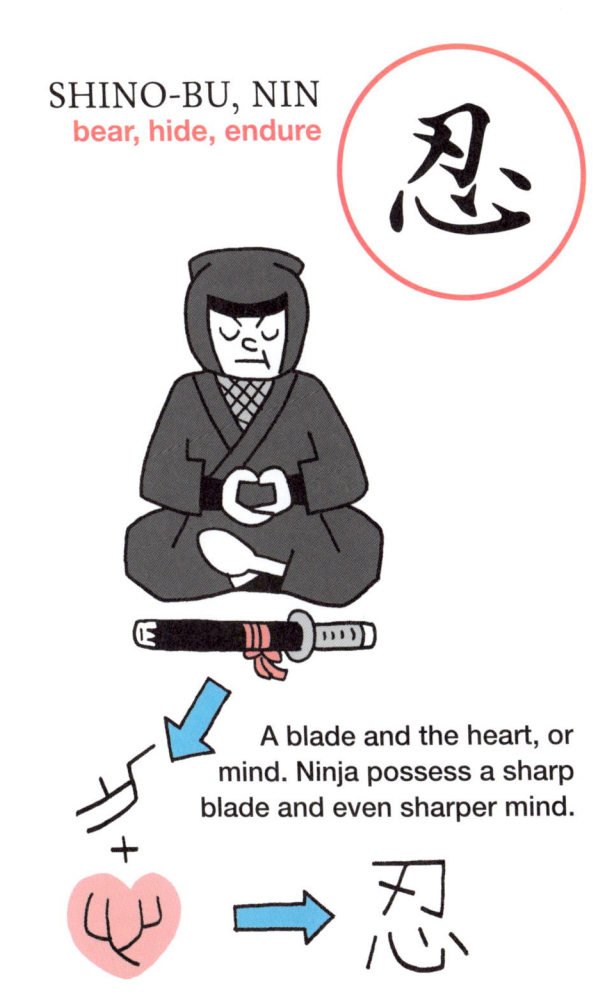

忍

A blade and the heart, or mind. Ninja possess a sharp blade and even sharper mind.

→ 忍

し の - ぶ

IKI
breath

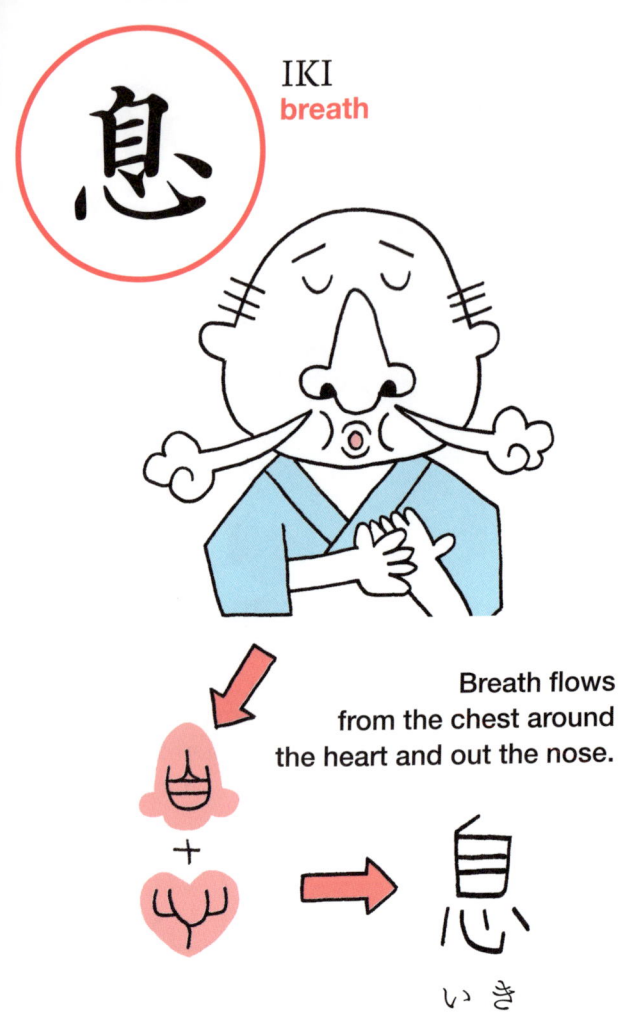

息

Breath flows from the chest around the heart and out the nose.

→ 息

いき

198

WASU-RERU
forget

忘

To forget is to have memories disappear from your mind.

亡 + ♥(心) → 忘

わす-れる

思

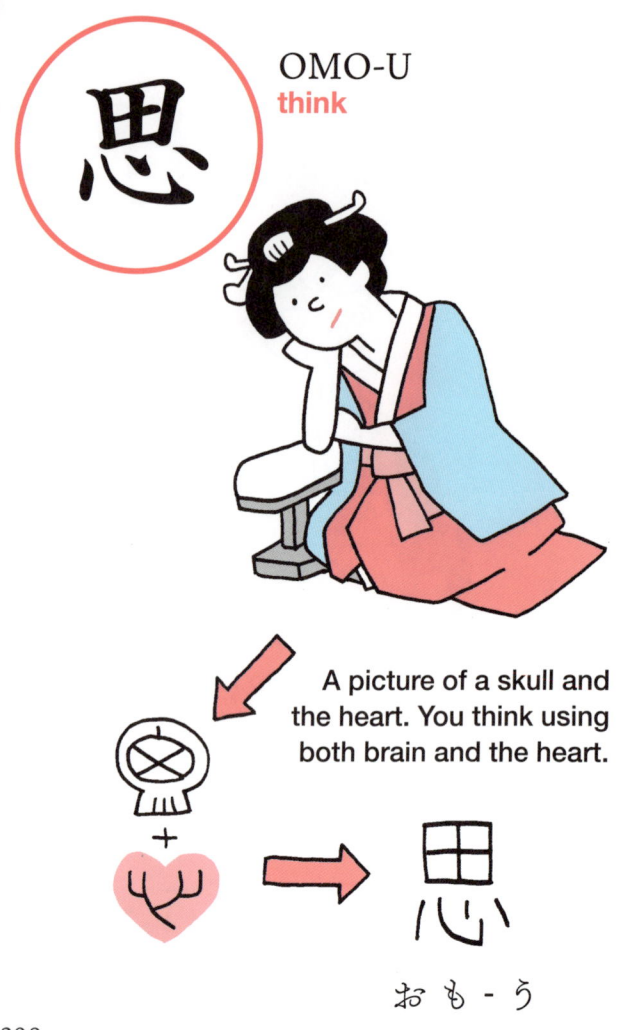

OMO-U
think

A picture of a skull and the heart. You think using both brain and the heart.

お も - う

INDEX

A

arrow	矢	53
ask	問	193
attach	付	189

B

back	背	134
bamboo	竹	91
beautiful	美	159
before	先	127
bell	鐘	124
big	大	97
bird	鳥	41
blade	刃	47
blow	吹	105
boat	舟	50
body	体	191
bone	骨	34
bow	弓	52
breath	息	198
bridge	橋	62
bright	明	83
bubble	泡	164
bug	虫	94

C

camellia	椿	186
capital city	京	66
car	車	49
cat	猫	156
center	中	72
change	化	100
character	文	71
cherry blossom	桜	94
child	子	29、62
chopsticks	箸	156
cloud	雲	124
compare	比	101
cooperation	協	139
correct	正	119
cow	牛	36
craft	工	48
cry	鳴	158
cut	切	174

D

death	死	141
desk	机	32
disappear	亡	129

disaster	災	88
dog	犬	35
door	戸	57
down	下	74
drink	飲	183

E

ear	耳	19、94
early	早	96
earth	土	13
eat	食	182
electricity	電	166
elephant	象	39
embarrassment	恥	137
end	末	79
endure	忍	197
energy	気	69
enter	入	169
evening	夕	84
every	毎	168
exit	出	120
eye	目	18

F

fall	落	186
field	畑	62
fire	火	15
fish	魚	42
fist	拳	115
flame	炎	87
flower	花	94、147
fly	飛	152
forest	森	77
forget	忘	199
friend	友	112
frog	蛙	32
fruit	果	82
fur	毛	44

G

garments	衣	68
gate	門	58
gather	集	153
go	行	65
goods	品	103
grass	草	149

H

half	半	151
hand	手	22
harmony	和	146
hear	聞	194
heart	心	26
heaven	天	98
heavy	重	180
high	高	67
hole	穴	170
horse	馬	38、94
house	家	62
hug	抱	196
husband	夫	156

I

ice	氷	162
inexpensive	安	167
inferior	劣	138

J

jewel	玉	54
jump	飛	32

L

leaf	葉	32
learn	学	171
left	左	111
leg	足	23
life	生	85
light	光	89
like	好	163
long	長	132

M

man	男	143
many	多	188
mask	面	135
match	合	176
meet	会	177
money	金	14
moon	月	9
mountain	山	6
mouth	口	20

N

name	名	104
not yet	未	80

O

| ogre | 鬼 | 133 |
| old | 古 | 140 |

P

part	分	173
persimmon	柿	124
person	人	27
plate	皿	55
pond	池	32
post	杭	94
power	力	24
progress	進	161
pull	引	175

Q

| quarrel | 争 | 114 |

R

rain	雨	16
receive	受	181
red	赤	186
relationship	仲	190
remember	覚	126
rest	休	128
rice	米	90
rice cake	餅	156
rice field	田	17
right	右	110
river	川	7
road	道	62
rock	石	12
root	本	78
rope	綱	94
run	走	117

S

sake	酒	156
same	同	178
save	保	192
say	言	106
scatter	散	94
see	見	121
self	自	21
sheep	羊	37
shell	貝	43
show	示	172
sky	空	124

small	小	150
smelly	臭	160
snow	雪	62、165
song	歌	109
sound	音	32、108
stand	立	99
star	星	86
stop	止	116
strike	当	144
suffer	苦	148
sun	日	8
sword	刀	46

T

take	取	136
talk	話	107
temple	寺	124
think	思	200
think	考	130
thread	糸	51
throw	投	195
together	共	113
tongue	舌	102
tool	具	179
tooth	歯	25
tower	塔	124
town	町	142
tree	木	11
troubled	困	81
turn	回	70
turtle	亀	40

U

up	上	73

V

village	村	62
volume	冊	59

W

walk	歩	118
water	水	10
well	井	56
white	白	186
wife	妻	156
window	窓	32
wings	羽	45
woman	女	28

woods	林	76
wrap	包	131

Y

yen	円	64

著者　ブレット・メイヤー（Bret Mayer）
1982年、アメリカのニュージャージー州で生まれる。現在静岡県浜松市在住。2012年の秋、非漢字文化圏外国人として初めて漢字検定一級に合格。それによって、漢字検定全級合格も達成。2013年の春には、立命館大学白川静記念東洋文字文化研究所から漢字教育士の資格を認定され、現在、外国人のみならず日本人へも、テレビやラジオ、インターネットを通じて漢字を教え、その魅力を伝えている。

装　丁	寄藤文平＋新垣裕子（文平銀座）
イラスト	いぢちひろゆき
編集協力	オフィス303、石村明淑
編集担当	斉藤正幸（ナツメ出版企画）

ナツメ社Webサイト
https://www.natsume.co.jp
書籍の最新情報（正誤情報を含む）は
ナツメ社Webサイトをご覧ください。

本書に関するお問い合わせは、書名・発行日・該当ページを明記の上、下記のいずれかの方法にてお送りください。電話でのお問い合わせはお受けしておりません。
・ナツメ社webサイトの問い合わせフォーム
　https://www.natsume.co.jp/contact
・FAX（03-3291-1305）
・郵送（下記、ナツメ出版企画株式会社宛て）
なお、回答までに日にちをいただく場合があります。正誤のお問い合わせ以外の書籍内容に関する解説・個別の相談は行っておりません。あらかじめご了承ください。

My First KANJI Book
Japanese Language and Culture through Pictures

2016年 6月30日	初版発行
2025年10月20日	第17刷発行

著 者	ブレット・メイヤー	Bret Mayer，2016
発行者	田村正隆	

発行所　株式会社ナツメ社
　　　　〒101-0051　東京都千代田区神田神保町1-52ナツメ社ビル1F
　　　　TEL　03-3291-1257（代表）　FAX　03-3291-5761
　　　　振替　00130-1-58661
制　作　ナツメ出版企画株式会社
　　　　〒101-0051　東京都千代田区神田神保町1-52ナツメ社ビル3F
　　　　TEL　03-3295-3921（代表）
印刷所　TOPPANクロレ株式会社

ISBN978-4-8163-6060-2　　　　©NATSUMESHA　　　　Printed in Japan
〈定価はカバーに表示してあります〉〈乱丁・落丁本はお取り替えします〉
本書の一部または全部を著作権法上で定められている範囲を超え、
ナツメ出版企画株式会社に無断で複写、複製、転載、データファイル化することを禁じます。